T0360849

Food Cultures and Geographical Indications in Norway

This book analyses the implementation and challenges of using Geographical Indications in Norway.

Adapting the modern and global system of Geographical Indications (GIs) to food cultures is a recurring challenge. This text uses Norway as a case study to describe, understand, and explain the socio-cultural adaptation of GIs. The empirical analysis shows that administrators, producers, consultants, and others make a significant effort to adapt the scheme to Norwegian food culture and the food culture to the scheme. Through the development and use of a new conceptual framework, the book continues to show how adaptations occurred and their influence on the development of the Norwegian food culture. The author also reflects upon the status of Norwegian GIs in emerging food cultural contexts related to sustainable and technology change. In summary, this book exhibits the connection between modern global legislative arrangements and traditional local products, providing a springboard for further research on cultural adaptation work of GIs in established and future global food cultures.

This book will be of interest to researchers, policymakers, and students in agri-food studies, sociology of food and agriculture, agricultural and rural development, and cultural studies.

Atle Wehn Hegnes is a researcher at Oslo Metropolitan University and the Norwegian Institute of Bioeconomy Research, Norway.

Routledge Focus on Environment and Sustainability

Ecohydrology-Based Landscape Restoration
Theory and Practice
Mulugeta Dadi Belete

Regional Political Ecologies and Environmental Conflicts in India
Edited by Sarmistha Pattanaik and Amrita Sen

Circular Economy and the Law
Bringing Justice into the Frame
Feja Lesniewska and Katrien Steenmans

Land Tenure Reform in Sub-Saharan Africa
Interventions in Benin, Ethiopia, Rwanda, and Zimbabwe
Steven Lawry, Rebecca McLain, Margaret Rugadya,
Gina Alvarado, and Tasha Heidenrich

Agricultural Digitization and Zhongyong Philosophy
Creating a Sustainable Circular Economy
Yiyan Chen, Hooi Hooi Lean, and Ye Li

EU Trade-Related Measures against Illegal Fishing
Policy Diffusion and Effectiveness in Thailand and Australia
Edited by Alin Kadfak, Kate Barclay, and Andrew M. Song

Food Cultures and Geographical Indications in Norway
Atle Wehn Hegnes

For more information about this series, please visit: www.routledge.com/ Routledge-Focus-on-Environment-and-Sustainability/book-series/RFES

Food Cultures and Geographical Indications in Norway

Atle Wehn Hegnes

LONDON AND NEW YORK

First published 2024
by Routledge
4 Park Square, Milton Park, Abingdon, Oxon OX14 4RN

and by Routledge
605 Third Avenue, New York, NY 10158

Routledge is an imprint of the Taylor & Francis Group, an informa business

British Library Cataloguing-in-Publication Data
A catalogue record for this book is available from the British Library

ISBN: 978-0-367-69729-7 (hbk)
ISBN: 978-0-367-69735-8 (pbk)
ISBN: 978-1-003-14302-4 (ebk)

DOI: 10.4324/9781003143024

Typeset in Times New Roman
by Newgen Publishing UK

Contents

Preface

Experience has shown that a range of challenges are related to how the modern global scheme of Geographical Indications for traditional food is adapted into national and local food contexts and cultures. Accompanying the challenge of adaptation of GIs to specific food cultural contexts is a need for a conceptual framework to understand how the work on food cultural adaptations takes place and the consequences it brings. The aim of this book is to contribute to the discussion of these challenges.

The substantial objective of the book is to describe how adaptation of GIs takes place through the empirical examples of preparations, administration, and the use of Geographical Indications in Norway. Additionally, it describes and discuss the consequences and implications of the food cultural adaptation work.

On a conceptual level, the book presents a tailored conceptual framework to understand how the scheme of GI is adapted to Norwegian food cultural conditions and how Norwegian food culture is adapted to the scheme. The system of concepts elucidates earlier contributions and can be constructively transferred to studies of GIs in other countries and food cultural contexts. Compared to existing literature, the book represents a novel contribution in mainly three areas:

1. It is the first holistic analysis of preparations, administration, and the use of Geographical Indications in Norway.
2. It reviews and relates to the international literature on how GIs are adapted in different national and local food cultures.

3. It presents a tailored conceptual framework of cultural adaptation work to analyze how GIs are implemented and adapted in different contexts and the consequences and implications this brings.

References to electronic sources, public documents, newspaper articles, and other resources are made continuously in endnotes and are compiled in separate overviews under the heading Research literature and other sources.

Acknowledgements

This book is mainly based on my PhD thesis in Norwegian from 2013[1] but is also informed by my research on GIs before and after the thesis was completed. I especially thank Anneli Olsbø for translating the chapter *The food-cultural adaptation work of Norwegian GIs* from Norwegian. *Consumption Research Norway* (SIFO) at Oslo Metropolitan University and *Norwegian Institute of Bioeconomy Research* (NIBIO) have been my academic homes and studies during the writing process. I'm grateful for the support from both institutes. I also thank colleagues, family, and friends for continuous backup and inspiration. Needless to say, I alone remain responsible for the content, the conclusions reached and the remaining errors and deficiencies in the book.

Note

1 Full text in Norwegian available at http://urn.nb.no/URN:NBN:no-38793

1 Introductions

Food cultures

Food cultures are at the same time stable while constantly evolving and adapting. The understanding of food cultures, and cultures in general, is therefore multifaceted and never fully clarified.

> In spite of the fact that European food culture has undergone a degree of normalization and that both the quantity and quality of food consumed are generally *socially* determined, these national distinctions endure. We encounter them in the literature and popular imagination of recent centuries, and they show no signs of disappearing. The peoples of the south – moderate, frugal, fond of the products of the earth and vegetable foods – are contrasted with those of the north, voracious and carnivorous. These are of course stereotypical characterizations, and make little sense if divorced from social variables. 'North' and 'south', for example, constitute an abstract geographical antithesis; they do not capture local varieties and cut horizontally across national distinctions.
>
> (Montanari 1994:110–111)

In his book *The Culture of Food* (1994), the renowned food historian Massimo Montanari understands food culture as a complex phenomenon composed of various levels of food cultures, spanning from the European to the local level. The quote serves as a constructive starting point for this book, which, seen through the prism of Geographical Indications, focuses on the adaptation of Norwegian food cultures to other food cultures. Furthermore,

DOI: 10.4324/9781003143024-1

Montanari's perspective invites Norwegian food culture to be placed within a broader European context and allows for a closer clarification of what is emphasised in the understanding of culture and food culture in this sociologically inspired study.

It belongs to the discourse of cultural sociology to adjust the meaning of the concept of culture to the culture in which we live and the cultures we study. In this sense, the concept of culture has also had various meanings, from referring to "The best that has been thought and known"[1] to "That complex whole"[2] and gradually evolving to today's emphasis on culture as the creation of meaning (Griswold 1994:3–13).

In this study, I understand culture and cultures primarily as:

ongoing (Hannerz 1992:4) meaning-making (Spillman 2002:4) processes (du Gay et al. 1997:3) of ideas and modes of thoughts (Hannerz 1992:7), related to structures of social relations (Hannerz 1992:264), physical objects (Griswold 1994:12) and how cultural complexity (Hannerz 1992) is interwoven with society (Griswold 1994:12) and characterized by a relative autonomy in shaping actions and institutions (Alexander and Smith 2003:12).

Beyond this synthesised and relatively established understanding of the concept of culture, I also stress that culture is characterised by various kinds of adaptation work. Food cultures thus also includes adaptation of (i) the meaning of food, (ii) the sociality of food, and (iii) the materiality of food. In other words, it includes how we adapt the way we understand the food we cook, eat, receive, or give away; how we adapt the groups we belong to in relation to how we understand food and how we make it; and, finally, what physical properties we give to food through its production and consumption. All these kinds of adaptations must be further understood in relation to the societal institutions and contextual conditions they are part of and relate to. In such an understanding of cultural and food cultural complexity, adaptations and their related processes are crucial. This requires studies of culture and food culture that focus on adaptive practices, what triggers them, how they occur, and what consequences and implications they bring. This study of the preparations, administration, and use of Geographical Indications in Norway represents such an analysis of culture and food cultures.

WTO, EU, Norway – The many faces of Geographical Indications

In the Agreement on Trade-Related Aspects of Intellectual Property Rights (TRIPS), The World Trade Organisation defines GIs as:

> [...] indications which identify a good as originating in the territory of a Member, or a region or locality in that territory, where a given quality, reputation or other characteristic of the good is essentially attributable to its geographical origin.[3]

Systems for GIs for foodstuff are implemented in various ways in different national laws, and the understanding and definition of GIs has been controversial on a WTO level for years (Josling 2006; Echols 2008; Geuze 2009). Whereas the US prefers trademark legislation and will not protect GIs with specific *sui generis* legislation, the EU already has such a system for GIs that they encourage other countries to implement. This will ideally give European products the same protection outside EU, as inside the union. In recent years the system of GIs has gained increased attention in international regions, such as Africa, Asia, and the Americas (CIRAD and FAO 2022; Bonanno, Sekine and Feuer 2019).

The common European system for PDO (Protected Designation of Origin) and PGI (Protected Geographical Indication) was established in 1992, inspired by existing national systems, e.g., the French AOC (Appellation d'Origine Contrôlée) and the Italian DOC (Denominazione d'Origine Controllata). The French AOC scheme is closely related to the notion of *terroir* (Barham 2003; Bérard and Marchenay 2008). A terroir product is historically related to a specific geographical origin through food culture and socio-ecological conditions. These factors are considered and evaluated in applications for an AOC/PDO/PGI label. However, there is an important difference between PDO and PGI, as described by Bérard and Marchenay:

> The philosophy behind PDO regulation is to protect, by means of a name, a unique product that cannot be reproduced in any other place. Production must be wholly confined to a specific geographical area and the product's characteristics must be

demonstrably connected with and influenced by that area. A PGI also protects a name but focuses mainly on a product's reputation, historical links with a given place and particular characteristics and qualities. The product need not be wholly manufactured within a specific geographical area: raw materials, in particular, may come from elsewhere.

(2008:14–15)

Toward the end of the 1980s, Norwegian governmental authorities and other key agri-food stakeholders started mobilising what came to be described as *mental border protection* (Hegnes and Amilien 2019). Simply put, the strategy aimed to trigger new ways of understanding food and to convince Norwegian consumers to choose Norwegian products. This Norwegian top-down turn to new qualities coincided with a growing turn to new qualities in Europe, characterised by a bottom-up initiative by consumers, retailers, and producers away from standardised products towards alternative qualities (Goodman 2003).

Positive experiences with similar schemes in EU countries were important for the introduction of GIs in Norway. In line with the new strategy, the regulations for GIs were set up in Norway modelled on corresponding systems in the EU and entered into force in July 2002.[4] However, no extensive tradition of designating products with their place of origin existed in Norway and there was lack of both a common vocabulary and food-cultural know-how in line with the food-cultural preconditions that form the basis for the GIs for food in the EU. In other words, the Norwegian food culture lacked a strong understanding and terminology to describe the dynamic trinity of products, peoples, and places, as in *terroir*. Since its introduction, the regulation has therefore resulted in significant work to adapt the scheme to Norwegian food culture, and Norwegian food culture to the scheme. The actors' work with adaptations of meaning, social organisation, and materiality, during preparations, administration, and use of the Norwegian scheme for GIs thus became important in the entrenchment of the scheme (Hegnes 2019).

Since its introduction, the labeling scheme has encouraged cooperation and resulted in increased recognition for several producer groups. As of May 2023, 35 Norwegian and 3 Italian products have a legally protected product designation in Norway.

The fruit villages in Hardanger on the Norwegian west coast have the most protected products, with protection for apples, apple cider, apple juice, pears, cherries, and plums. The recruiting of new products is still ongoing and the work on adapting control systems and revising existing product regulations is important to ensure the scheme's legitimacy among both users and consumers. However, studies of the Norwegian context and Norwegian consumers' conceptions of local food have found that few consumers understand food along the terroir dimensions in Norway (Amilien et al. 2008; Haugrønning et al. 2018).[5]

The challenges of adapting Geographical Indications

Adaptations are a repeated theme in research on GIs. There are many that claim, and demonstrate, that adaptations of various kinds are necessary in order for GI-schemes to function constructively in different countries and food cultures. Adaptations are described using terms such as *translations* (Millet 2019; Cappeliez 2017; Barham 2003; Bérard and Marchenay 2006:110; Feagan 2007:37; Fonte and Grando 2006:44,49; Marty 1997:54; Bérard and Marchenay 1996:240; Rangnekar 2004:22; Marsden et al. 2000:425–426; Renting et al. 2003:400), *reorganisations* (Crescenzi et al. 2022:387; Millet et al. 2020; Martino et al. 2018:21; Rangnekar 2004:4), and *transformations* (Bardone and Spalvēna 2019; Mariani et al. 2021:472; Ray 1998:9–10; Tregear et al. 2007:13; Bérard and Marchenay 2007; Vakoufaris 2010:39; Marsden et al. 2000:30; Marescotti 2003:4).

The overall strength of the international contributions is that they identify and describe a range of factors that need to be adapted and how this is done. However, the complex diversity of adaptation needs and adaptive practices that the contributions identify overall is not systematically problematised, nor nuanced. In general, conceptual distinctions are not made, even where different terms such as translation, reorganisation, and transformation are employed to describe different kinds of adaptations. The terms are often used as more or less arbitrary and interchangeable labels for actions or refer to processes where something is changed or altered into something else. In general, the focus is on one or a few of the many adaptations and possible practices associated with them. The significance of adaptations themselves is not studied as a separate and important phenomenon and a conceptual framework is not established that makes it possible to identify, understand, and describe why adaptations arise, who performs them, what characterises them, how they relate and what consequences and implications they have. This has left the concrete adaptation work that is at play unclear.

With a lack of relevant conceptual tools to conduct a holistic analysis of the GIs in the Norwegian food culture, it was necessary to establish a more nuanced system of concepts.

Elements, dimensions, and dynamics in cultural adaptation work

The actor's overall adaptation work can be understood as the sum of the practices that takes place in the interplay between people's translations of language and knowledge, reorganisation of social relationships and transformation of material conditions and products. Administrators of the scheme in the Ministry of Agriculture and Food, the Norwegian Food Safety Authority and The Norwegian Agricultural Quality System and Food Branding Foundation take into consideration both the WTO's and EU's body of rules, at the same time as they also adapt the scheme into a Norwegian context and local Norwegian food culture. Correspondingly, food producers adapt their traditions and products to the new regulation's conditions. Hence, the adaptation practices have significance beyond being adaptations of language and knowledge, social relationships, and the materiality. When they are used to adapt the relationship between global and modern rules and traditional local products, they become simultaneously strategies and actions, which makes it possible to adapt the global to the local, tradition to innovation and vice versa.

The system of concepts developed in the analysis of the Norwegian case, elucidates earlier scientific perspectives. The mutual work on adaptation of the scheme to Norwegian food culture, and the Norwegian food culture to the scheme, is understood as *Cultural Adaptation Work* (CAW) and constitutes the core element in the system of concepts established. Further, this new system of concepts is specifically tailored to analyse different cultural differences, actors, knowledge and adaptation skills, adaptation practices, dimensions, power relations and contextual conditions, from which adaptation work can be understood. The framework makes it possible to identify, understand, and describe how the adaptations take place, who carries them out, what characterises them, and what consequences and implications they have. This perspective opens for a range and variety of practices. In this analysis I have mainly focused on three of them:

- *Translations* are the work exerted to create changes and adaptations of meaning, e.g., relating to the labelling scheme and product regulations. Translation occurs when new meaning arises or is being changed. Through the adaptation work the meaning of places, products, and brands is created.
- *Reorganisations* are changes in social relations and groups or the creation of new groups. Reorganisation can occur both at the individual, group, and nation level. In addition, reorganisation occurs in both real groups, such as the formation of producer associations and groups on paper,[6] as they are constructed by researchers, market analysts, politicians, and others. Both forms of reorganisation are important and there is interaction between them. Real groups give rise to groups on paper, and vice versa.
- *Transformations* are innovations or changes of material conditions. Transformation is related to the material aspect of labelling schemes, and mainly the products. In addition to the products, means of production and a more general understanding of nature can also be taken as a basis for transformation.

The adaptive practices form an interplay, in which the different practices affect each other. Adapted regulations involve reorganisation of producers, who then change their products, and so on. The interplay is embedded in the tension between the global and the local, the old and the new, as shown in Figure 1.1.

The conceptual framework represents an analytical-methodological toolbox for analysing cultural adaptation work. In Table 1.1, I present an overview given in tabular form of its elements. The column on the left represents general elements in analysis of cultural adaptation work. In the middle column I compile the specific questions that can be asked in such analysis. The right column is specifically linked to the study of GIs in Norway and consists of the answers to the questions arising from the elements.

Figure 1.1 Model for Dimensions and Dynamics in Adaptation Work.

Table 1.1 Elements, Questions and Results in Studies of Cultural Adaptation Work

Elements	Questions	Results
Cultural differences	*What kind of cultural differences are there?*	• Different meaning • Different social organisation • Different material conditions
Actors	*Which actors are important for the adaptation work?*	• Public servants • Producers • Consultants
Knowledge and adaptation competence	*What kind of knowledge and adaptation competence do the actors have?*	• Knowledge about the legal system • Tacit knowledge • Adaptation competence
Adaptation practices	*What kind of adaptation practices are in play?*	• Translations • Reorganizations • Transformations
Dimensions	*Which dimensions can be related to the adaptation work?*	• Global/local • Tradition/innovation
Power	*What kind of power relations can be found?*	• Power shifts
Contexts	*What kind of historical, geographical, and institutional contexts are relevant?*	• The Quality Turn • WTO/EU/Norway/local • Law, economy, science, technology, politics.

This framework constitutes the methodological-analytical frame for the empirical analysis in the next chapter on the preparations, administration, and the use of Geographical Indications in Norway.

Analytical approach and methods

This analysis of Norwegian GI is based on diverse forms of empirical material. The starting point for the study was a wish to describe and understand how the scheme for protected designations was prepared and subsequently administrated and used in Norway based on existing schemes in the EU. During the data collection and analysis, it became clear that administrators, producers, consultants, and others make a significant and all-round effort to adapt the scheme to Norwegian food culture, and Norwegian food culture to the scheme. My identification of this work, its scope and significance, was important in terms of my decision to make people's work on cultural adaptation the main concern of the study.

Document studies of laws, policy documents, etc. have been analysed to uncover what kind of measures and concepts have been important for implementation of the scheme in Norway. Interviews with producer organisations have involved the persons responsible for working out product regulations in producer organisations. Interviews have also been conducted with consultants and key informants representing public administrative bodies administering the regulation. All interviews have been semi-structured. The interviews were conducted in August and September 2007, and February, March, June, and July 2008. Twenty-two interviews were conducted with a total of 30 people.

Notes

1 Griswold refers to Matthew Arnold (1822–1888) as representing this perspective on culture.
2 Griswold refers to Johann Gottfried Herder (1744–1803) as representing this perspective on culture.
3 Article 22 Protection of Geographical Indications, p. 328.
4 FOR 2002-07-05 no. 698: Regulation No 698 of 5 July 2002 on the Protection of Designations of Origin, Geographical Indications

and Designations of Specific Traditional Character of Agricultural Foodstuffs (hereafter; *Framework regulation*).

5 This section is mainly based on the introduction of "The map and the terroir" (Hegnes 2019).

6 Groups on paper can be understood in line with Bourdieu and Hacking's understanding of theoretical classes as "classes on paper" (Bourdieu 1985:725) and classifying people as "making up people" (Hacking 2007).

Research literature and other sources

Research publications

Alexander, J. C. and Smith, P. (2003) 'The Strong Program in Cultural Sociology – Elements of a Structural Hermeneutics', in Alexander, J. C. *The Meaning of Social Life – A Cultural Sociology* (pp. 11–26). New York: Oxford University Press.

Amilien, V., Schjøll, A. and Vramo, L. M. (2008) *Forbrukernes forståelse av lokal mat* (Fagrapport no. 1). Torshov: SIFO.

Bardone, E. and Spalvēna, A. (2019) 'European Union Food Quality Schemes and the Transformation of Traditional Foods into European Products in Latvia and Estonia', *Appetite*, 135: 43–53.

Barham, E. (2003) 'Translating Terroir: The Global Challenge of French AOC labeling', *Journal of Rural Studies,* 19: 127–138.

Bérard, L. and Marchenay, P. (1996) 'Tradition, Regulation and Intellectual Property: Local Agricultural Products and Foodstuffs in France', in Brush, S. B. and Stabinsky, D. (eds.) *Valuing Local Knowledge: Indigenous People and Intellectual Property Rights* (pp. 230–243). Washington, DC: Island Press.

Bérard, L. and Marchenay, P. (2006) 'Local Products and Geographical Indications: Taking Account of Local Knowledge and Biodiversity', *International Social Science Journal,* 58: 109–116.

Bérard, L. and Marchenay, P. (2007) 'Localized Products in France: Definition, Protection and Value-Adding', *Anthropology of Food,* http://aof.revues.org/415.

Bérard, L. and Marchenay, P. (2008) *From Localized Products to Geographical Indications. Awareness and Action.* Bourg-en-Bresse: CNRS Ressources des terroirs.

Bonanno, K., Sekine, K. and Feuer H. N. (eds.) (2019) *Geographical Indication and Global Agri-Food: Development and Democratization.* New York: Routledge.

Bourdieu, P. (1985) 'The Social Space and the Genesis of Groups', *Theory and Society,* 14: 723–744.

Cappeliez, S. (2017) 'How Well Does Terroir Travel? Illuminating Cultural Translation Using a Comparative Wine Case Study'. *Poetics*, 65: 24–36.

CIRAD and FAO (2022) *Worldwide perspectives on geographical indications.* Proceedings – Short papers, An International Conference for Researchers, Policy Makers and Practitioners Montpellier (France), 5–8 July 2022.

Crescenzi, R., De Filippis, F., Giua, M. and Vaquero-Piñeiro, C. (2022) 'Geographical Indications and Local Development: The Strength of Territorial Embeddedness', *Regional Studies*, 56: 381–393

du Gay, P., Hall, S., Janes, L. Mackay, H. and Negus, K. (1997) *Doing Cultural Studies: The Story of the Sony Walkman.* London: Sage.

Echols, M. A. (2008) *Geographical Indications for Food Products – International Legal and Regulatory Perspectives.* Austin: Wolters Kluwer Law & Business.

Feagan, R. (2007) 'The Place of Food: Mapping out the "Local" in Local Food Systems', *Progress in Human Geography,* 31: 23–42.

Fonte, M. and Grando, S. (2006) *A Local Habitation and a Name – Local Food and Knowledge Dynamics in Sustainable Rural Development.* WP6 CORASON – Local food production, comparative report 2 August. 2nd version.

Geuze, M. (2009) 'The Provisions on Geographical Indications in the TRIPS Agreement', *Estey Centre Journal of International Law and Trade Policy*, 10: 50–64.

Goodman, D. (2003) 'The Quality "Turn" and Alternative Food Practices: Reflections and Agenda', *Journal of Rural Studies,* 19: 1–7.

Griswold, W. (1994) *Cultures and Societies in a Changing World.* Thousand Oaks, Calif.: Pine Forge Press.

Hacking, I. (2007) 'Kinds of People: Moving Targets', *Proceedings of the British Academy,* 151: 285–318.

Hannerz, U. (1992) *Cultural Complexity: Studies in the Social Organization of Meaning.* New York: Columbia University Press.

Haugrønning, V., Amilien, V. and Roos, G. (2018) *Quality Labels Lost in Everyday Food Consumption – An Ethnographic Study of Six Norwegian Households Food Practices Linked To Food Quality Schemes and Sustainable Food Chains*, Project Note No. 8–2018, Consumption research Norway (SIFO) OsloMet. Oslo: Oslo Metropolitan University.

Hegnes, A. W. (2019) 'The Map and the Terroir: Adapting Geographical Boundaries for PDO and PGI in Norway ', *British Food Journal* 121(12): 3024–3042.

Hegnes, A. W. and Amilien, V. (2019) 'Geographical Indications – A Double-Edged Tool for Food Democracy: The Cases of the Norwegian Geographical Indication Evolution and the Protection of Stockfish from Lofoten as Cultural Adaptation Work', in Bonanno, A., Sekine, K. and Feuer H. N. (eds.) *Geographical Indication and Global Agri-Food: Development and Democratization* (pp. 100–117). New York: Routledge.

Josling, T. (2006) 'Presidential Address – The War on Terroir: Geographical Indications as a Transatlantic Trade Conflict', *Journal of Agricultural Economics,* 57: 337–363.

Marescotti, A. (2003) *Typical Products and Rural Development: Who Benefits from PDO/PGI recognition?* Paper presented at Food Quality Products in the Advent of the 21st Century: Production, Demand and Public Policy. 83rd EAAE Seminar, Chania, Greece, 4–7 September.

Mariani, M., Cerdan, C. and Peri, I. (2021) 'Origin Food Schemes and the Paradox of Reducing Diversity to Defend It', *Sociologia Ruralis,* 61: 465–490.

Marsden, T., Banks, J. and Bristow, G. (2000) 'Food Supply Chain Approaches: Exploring Their Role in Rural Development', *Sociologia Ruralis,* 4: 424–438.

Martino, G., Toccaceli, D. and Bavorova, M. (2018) 'An Analysis of Food Safety Private Investments Drivers in the Italian Meat Sector', *Agricultural Economics*, 65: 21–30.

Marty, F. (1997) 'Which are the Ways of Innovation in PDO and PGI Products?', in Arfini, F. and Mora, C. (eds.) *Typical and Traditional Products: Rural effect and Agro-Industrial Problems* (pp. 41–58). 52nd EAAE Seminar in Parma (19–21.6.1997): Parma.

Millet, M. (2019) 'From Ossau and Iraty to PDO Ossau-Iraty: The Long-Term Construction of a Product Based on Two Distinct Places', *British Food Journal*, 121: 3062–3075.

Millet, M., Keast, V., Gonano, S., and Casabianca, F. (2020) 'Product Qualification as a Means of Identifying Sustainability Pathways for Place-Based Agri-Food Systems: The Case of the GI Corsican Grapefruit (France)', *Sustainability*, *12*(17), 7148. MDPI AG.

Montanari, M. (1994) *The Culture of Food.* Oxford: Blackwell Publishers.

Rangnekar, D. (2004) *The Socio-Economics of Geographical Indications: A Review of Empirical Evidence from Europe.* Issue Paper No. 8. Geneva: UNCTAD-ICTSD Project on IPRs and Sustainable Development.

Ray, C. (1998) 'Culture, Intellectual Property and Territorial Rural Development', *Sociologia Ruralis,* 38: 3–20.

Renting, H., Marsden, T. K. and Banks, J. (2003) 'Understanding Alternative Food Networks: Exploring the Role of Short Supply Chains in Rural Development', *Environment and Planning A,* 35: 393–411.

Spillman, L. (2002) 'Introduction: Culture and Cultural Sociology', in Spillman, L. (ed.) *Cultural Sociology* (pp. 1–15). Malden, Mass.: Blackwell.

Tregear, A., Arfini, F., Belletti, G. and Marescotti, A. (2007) 'Regional Foods and Rural Development: The Role of Product Qualification', *Journal of Rural Studies,* 23: 12–22.

Vakoufaris, H. (2010) 'The Impact of Ladotyri Mytilinis PDO Cheese on the Rural Development of Lesvos island, Greece', *Local Environment,* 15: 27–41.

Regulations

Agreement on Trade-Related Aspects of Intellectual Property Rights, 15 April 1994, Marrakesh Agreement Establishing the World Trade Organization, Annex 1C, 33 ILM 1197, pp. 319–351.

2 The food-cultural adaptation work of Norwegian GIs

Cultural adaptation work is about harmonising cultural differences by adapting different cultural components to each other. My analysis of the preparations, administration, and use of geographical indications focuses on such work and on how it is expressed at different times, in different locations and what consequences it has.

The adaptation work in the preparations, administration and use of geographical indications could be analysed in different ways. Parts of the development, described under the heading preparations and implementations, could have been discussed under the heading administration, and topics dealt with under administration could have been discussed under use. The reason for choosing to distinguish between different phases is that it reflects the issue at hand. The fact that sub-analyses overlap with each other serves as a reminder of the fluid and relational nature of adaptation work.

Not all findings in each sub-analysis will necessarily represent fundamentally new knowledge. Some of the topics have previously been studied separately. The presentation is to some extent influenced by the development and use of the system of concepts. However, the chronology of the historical process has had a bearing on how the presentation is structured. Another important comment on the form of presentation is that it is not a systematic case-by-case review. The best or most instructive sub-cases have been selected to shed light on the common characteristics I wish to emphasise.

The analysis comprises three sub-analyses and a concluding summary, in addition to this section on the intentions behind it.

DOI: 10.4324/9781003143024-2

The first sub-analysis largely consists of a review of the period until Norway introduced its labelling scheme for PDO, PGI, and TSG. This historical review is primarily based on data from documents. In the second sub-analysis, I deal with adaptation work in the administration of the Norwegian labelling scheme. This analysis is based on both documents and interviews. The analysis of use is largely limited to the producers and producer organisations affiliated to the scheme. The final sub-analysis is mainly based on interviews.

Preparations and implementation of Geographical indications in Norway

> After the trip, the participants are expected to have acquired a knowledge base that will enable them to lead the work of implementing a system for origin labelling of agricultural products in Norway.[1]

Introduction

In this sub-analysis, I will follow the process from when the idea of a labelling scheme first arose in Norway in the late 1980s until the scheme was adopted on 5 July 2002. The Norwegian scheme for PDO, PGI, and TSG is one of several examples of measures and new ways of thinking about new food qualities in Norway during this period. This presentation therefore alternates between circumstances specifically linked to the Norwegian labelling scheme and a more general understanding of the quality turn. In this way, I will show how the Norwegian scheme influences and is influenced by the specific context of which the scheme was, and still is, a part. Overall, I will show how the introduction of the Norwegian GI scheme depended on cultural adaptation work.

The specialty foods are imbued with meaning by virtue of being special, for example by being presented as different from bulk products. In 2009, Minister of Agriculture and Food Lars Peder Brekk said the following about the relationship between these two categories:

> The production of speciality foods provides an opportunity to achieve good prices in the market and to preserve

Norwegian food traditions and food culture! It is the local products that make the 'Taste of Norway' food strategy possible! The grocery chains and the food industry have made the most of these possibilities by reducing their focus on cheap bulk products and concentrating more on niche foods and specialities.[2]

The quality turn stands in contrast to the period when the bulk regime dominated, which may have *contributed to an 'un-learning' of taste literacy among Norwegian consumers* (Jacobsen 1999:10). The Norwegian labelling scheme for PDO, PGI, and TSG, on the other hand, is based on a particular taste literacy and an understanding that origin and quality are closely linked. This recognition and mentality when it comes to food requires food-cultural adaptation and revival work to relearn the knowledge that was unlearnt under the bulk regime.

The analysis spans the period from the present back to Gro Harlem Brundtland's second government (1986–1989), in which Gunhild Øyangen (Labour) served as Minister of Agriculture. Three factors go hand in hand in the preparatory works to and the introduction of the Norwegian GI scheme. They concern how the scheme is to be financed, organised and translated from the EU. Until the scheme's establishment in 2002, these are the main factors that the adaptation work focuses on. Translations and reorganisations are the key practices in the work of introducing and adapting the Norwegian GI scheme to the European regulatory framework and the Norwegian context and food culture. The result of this adaptation work forms the basis for the transformation work that is triggered once the scheme is in place.

The dawn of a green starting point for niche products

Some of the first vague beginnings of the quality turn and what was to become the Norwegian labelling scheme for PDO, PGI, and TSG can be found in a 1989 proposition to the Norwegian Parliament, the Storting:

One will propose to the Norwegian Agricultural Marketing Board that more of the funds used for sales promotion be allocated to developing new products and new markets.[3]

It is of course difficult to identify the exact origins of the ideas about a Norwegian GI scheme at this early stage. There are many and diverse sources. The above quotation implies that the quality turn depends on adaptative practices. *Developing new products and new markets* requires adaptation work in the form of both transformations and reorganisations. Looking back at this specific measure proposed in 1989 helps us to understand that it forms part of the early development of the quality turn. This is made even clearer in another proposition to the Storting dated the following year,[4] in which agricultural products and markets are divided into three categories. Organic and niche products are mentioned as two concrete product types and markets that the marketing efforts should focus on. The decisive reason why they are mentioned separately is that they are distinct from each other and from other agricultural products, which can implicitly be understood to refer to bulk or industrial products.

At this time, organic products and organic quality appear to be more clearly defined and understood than what falls within the rather unspecified category *other niche products*. Part of the explanation for this is that Debio was established as a private organisation as early as 1986. Debio was charged with checking, approving and labelling organic products with the Ø label, which became the label for products certified by Debio.

The distinction between different agricultural products and qualities that was beginning to emerge at this time still exists today. Adaptation work has been an important part of the quality turn in that it established distinctions and organised these food qualities in relation to each other.

In 1990, the Standing Committee on Agriculture submitted a concrete proposal for a dedicated strategy based on environmentally friendly principles:

> The Committee also wishes to emphasise that environmentally friendly forms of farming must increasingly be given a place throughout the agricultural system. The Committee will ask the Ministry to consider a strategy for 'Clean Food' that covers all links in the chain, from producer to consumer.[5]

Environmentally friendly and clean production was already in focus before the launch of the *Clean Food* strategy. However, sometimes ideas about food qualities other than the purely environmental aspect can also be found here and in other preparatory works. The Official Norwegian Report (NOU) *Norsk landbrukspolitikk – Utfordringer, mål and virkemidler* ('Norwegian Agricultural Policy – Challenges, goals and policy instruments' – in Norwegian only), which was submitted to the Ministry of Agriculture on 11 December 1990,[6] contains an example of how ideas about the local and the traditional aspects of products were highlighted as potential Norwegian quality resources. In the Official Norwegian Report, clean, organic national and local processing traditions are presented as resources for the Norwegian agriculture of the future.[7] Organic production is already known, so it is natural that it is emphasised. Local processing traditions seem almost to be subsumed by the clean category or are somewhat overshadowed by this quality. In this perspective, you could say that the focus on niche products grew out of the green wave. In addition to the focus on environmental and local qualities, the food is implicitly linked to a time dimension. To put it simply, we can say that there is a distinction between traditional foods and modern or industrial bulk foods.

A proposition to the Storting regarding amendments of the national budget for 1991 contains a section where it emerges that the Clean Food strategy is taking shape, entitled *Strategi for "renmat" – markedsundersøkelser for eksport* ('Strategy for "Clean Food" – market surveys for export' – in Norwegian only). More and more factors and quality dimensions are mentioned in the preparatory work to the strategy, in addition to *environmentally friendly forms of operation*. Examples include health, quality, product development, market surveys, export and that *[a]mong other things, it will be important to analyse the link between production and product quality in greater detail*.[8] Although the main focus is on Norwegian quality in general, the above quotation suggests an opening for food qualities as they have since come to be understood in relation to the Norwegian scheme for PDO, PGI, and TSG.

To summarise, we see a slowly emerging focus on the relationship between place, tradition, and product quality during the early days of the quality turn. The turn makes slow progress. National bulk remains the prevailing quality dimension. The clean or organic aspect attracts more attention than the other new qualities, and the understanding of niche products and markets develops on the basis of this quality.

The national aspect strikes back

The proposition to the Storting entitled *Landbruk i utvikling*[9] ('Agriculture in development' – in Norwegian only) also describes the new Clean Food strategy as 'Competitive Strategies for Norwegian Food (KOSTRAT)', and describes it as one of three main areas in the competitive strategy the government was developing for the organised sale of food.[10] *Agriculture in development* also seems to take a step back as regards the focus on local and traditional food. The national level is again highlighted and emphasised (pp. 29–30). Which qualities the *Clean Food strategy* should focus on thus alternate between the general and national level, on the one hand, and the special and local, on the other. The final strategy is open to both approaches, however. The long-term results of this include the national labelling scheme *Godt Norsk* and the Norwegian scheme for PDO, PGI, and TSG.

The discussions of labelling schemes during the initial period of the quality turn focused on a common national quality, but there are also signs of adaptation work. Clean Food and KOSTRAT emerged partly in response to the possibility of Norway joining the EU. The adaptation to a more open market consisted of identifying and adapting qualities to focus on in future, as described, e.g., by Nygård and Storstad (1998:40).

The development of the new qualities during this period can be described as two steps forward and one step back. Despite the 'return' to the focus on national quality, the new qualities continue to make themselves felt.

The new qualities emerge

Looking back at the preparatory works and the final Clean Food strategy, we can see the seed of what was to become the Norwegian scheme for PDO, PGI, and TSG. A labelling scheme for Norwegian products was highlighted as an important measure. The objective was *to develop and establish a labelling scheme for Norwegian quality products based on Norway's competitive advantages.*[11] The examples cited of such advantages specify *products based on local food traditions*[12] and *old Norwegian food traditions/food culture and similar.*[13]

The *Godt Norsk* foundation was established in February 1994 as a result of KOSTRAT. The foundation was assigned responsibility for the labelling scheme with the same name that was intended to promote Norwegian quality.[14] When the *Godt Norsk* scheme was established, it was not entirely clear which qualities the scheme would include. Norwegian raw materials and production were the primary requirements, but old Norwegian food traditions/food culture etc. were also mentioned. However, the latter qualities remained less important than the focus on Norwegianness. Despite the fact that they were not yet fully formed at this stage, it is worth noting that such qualities were already considered a potential advantage ten years before the Norwegian scheme for PDO, PGI, and TSG was established. Another important aspect of the new strategy is its emphasis on the future labelling scheme (*Godt Norsk*) being adapted to both national and international conditions.[15]

Awareness of the importance of adapting Norwegian circumstances to other countries increases. Tension arises between the international and the national, and cultural adaptation practices are activated. The labelling scheme must be harmonised with the existing national context, but at the same time it is pointed out that it is being developed in an international context where international requirements and obligations must be taken into consideration. Nygård and Storstad also refer to this tension between the global, the national, the regional, and the local when choosing to use *Godt Norsk* as an example of the de-globalisation of food markets (1998:49). It is at this intersection between globalisation and de-globalisation that adaptation work arises and is practised.

The adaptation work was thus already present while KOSTRAT was being planned and the *Godt Norsk* labelling scheme was being developed. Reorganisations and translations of international requirements for labelling schemes had implications for the adaptation of *Godt Norsk*. Nevertheless, it was Norwegian quality and food culture that were most important in this adaptation work.

Budding awareness of the EU scheme

The idea of using geographical indications is explicitly described in the 1996 report *Effektiv matsikkerhet* ('Efficient food safety' – in Norwegian only).[16] Initially, it was only the possibility for Norwegian products to apply for protection under the EU system that was considered, but it was clear that the idea of introducing such schemes had been around for some time. This is evident from the fact that two concrete products are mentioned as potential candidates for the scheme, specifically the fermented fish product *Rakfisk* and *Gamalost* cheese. It is interesting to observe that the products mentioned are not linked to a specific place at this time, which would have been natural considering the scheme's focus on this aspect. If that link had been made explicitly, the products would have been referred to as *Rakfisk fra Valdres* (Rakfisk from Valdres) and *Gamalost frå Vik* (Gamalost from Vik). Both these products were later granted protection under the Norwegian scheme for PDO, PGI, and TSG as protected geographical indications in October and November 2006, respectively. The purely legal consequences of such regulations for Norway, exemplified by the general designation *geitost* ('goat cheese'), are also discussed. The goat cheese example also underlines the idea of labelling products without linking them to a local area, but to Norway as a whole. The fact that none of the products are linked to a limited geographical area in Norway and that labelling products based on nationality is also mentioned can be interpreted as a sign that it was still difficult to fully take on board the implications of the new way of thinking about food.

The *Efficient Food Safety* report was followed up with a white paper the following year that discussed food labelling regulations in general terms and with the focus on consumer needs.[17] The work of adapting provisions to national as well as international conditions is a recurring topic. Harmonisation and communication between actors are two of several ways of referring to this adaptation work. Both the concrete adaptation work and further planning of a new labelling scheme are given increasing attention as awareness of the phenomenon grows.

The government's wish to protect designations in Norway

Three years after the *Efficient Food Safety* report, the government wanted to establish a Norwegian GI scheme corresponding to the one already established in the EU. This is stated in Report No 19 to the Storting (1999–2000) *Om norsk landbruk and matproduksjon*

('On Norwegian agriculture and food production' – in Norwegian only).[18] Increased diversity in agricultural production is considered a positive way of highlighting regions and making the agricultural sector more exciting and attractive. The section on the future labelling scheme concludes that a more detailed study is needed of the organisational and financial aspects and legislation before such a labelling scheme can be established. As regards legislation, the white paper also mentions upcoming WTO negotiations (turn of the year 1999–2000) about the TRIPS Agreement and intellectual property rights. Reference is made to the fact that the negotiations will cover increased protection of what are known as geographical indications.[19] The section also shows that there is a stronger focus on regional and traditional aspects at the expense of national aspects, which were previously the main focus. Taken together, the examples show how the future labelling scheme for traditional local products will be adapted to a global regulatory framework.

Consumer orientation and construction

The Norwegian everyday connoisseur has been the figurehead for the quality turn. The notion of Norwegian consumers being particularly concerned with high quality and diversity and indifferent to price has been a necessary part of the effort to legitimise and justify the focus on speciality foods. When the Norwegian everyday connoisseur is used as evidence that everyone wants speciality foods, that is also a way of safeguarding a vulnerable Norwegian agricultural sector that depends on Norwegians buying Norwegian produce. Before, during and after the introduction of the Norwegian scheme for PDO, PGI, and TSG, the public authorities and market analysis companies endeavoured to establish a market for such products. They had to identify producers, consumers, and distribution channels that were consistent with the idea behind the quality turn. New categories such as 'speciality food producer', 'foodie consumers', and 'speciality foods' emerged during this period. Consumer orientation is therefore as much about constructing consumers or a market as it is about orienting marketing towards them. It can therefore be argued that some aspects of the consumer orientation have contributed to the adaptation work relating to the Norwegian GI scheme. On paper, consumers are organised by actors that want to know who buys their products, and perhaps also by the consumers themselves.

The above-mentioned white paper on Norwegian agriculture and food production (No 19, 1999–2000) also points to different motivations for establishing a GI labelling scheme. The focus on consumer orientation is one of them. The white paper points out that consumers want information about the origins of products and that they want to be able to choose products from particular regions or distinctive traditional products. It is emphasised that such a labelling scheme would not just provide consumers with information about where their food comes from, but also ensure that the products are original and subject to control.

The planning of the Norwegian system for PDO, PGI, and TSG coincided with this consumer orientation from the early 2000s.[20] Silje Rem mentions this link between labelling schemes and consumer orientation in the chapter 'Å stemme med gaffelen – Vendingen mot forbrukerne i norsk matpolitikk' ('Voting with your fork – the shift towards consumers in Norwegian food policy' – in Norwegian only). She writes as follows: *The authorities cannot exclude foreign products from the market to the same extent as before, but they nevertheless try to safeguard the domestic agricultural sector by influencing consumers to choose Norwegian products. [...] Examples include the previous Godt Norsk label and the introduction of the Norwegian scheme for PDO, PGD and TSG* (Rem 2008:44, 63).[21] Rem emphasises labelling schemes as means of increasing the consumption of Norwegian agricultural products. According to her description, however, there is also reason to claim that what is taking place is a 'correction' that takes account of producers as well as consumers.

The organisational and financial aspects and the meaning behind the EU regulations are three factors it became relevant to adapt after the decision had been made to introduce a GI labelling scheme in Norway. This makes mapping what needs to be reorganised and translated an important part of the further adaptation work. Consumer orientation is also an important trend which takes place, among other things, by labelling new qualities.

Adaptation work intensified

The *Godt Norsk* foundation's (SGN) annual report for 1999 (p. 8) describes a study the foundation carried out in collaboration with the Norwegian Trade Council under the heading *Opprinnelsesmerking* ('origin labelling'). It was still somewhat unclear what a Norwegian GI scheme would entail, but it is clear that translating the EU system was being considered. This is evident, for example, in the sentence where the study is described as being *carried out in accordance with the labelling schemes set out in EU regulations.* One of the motives mentioned is that such a scheme will help to *differentiate the products from imported products.* In retrospect, however, there is reason to point out that the task of distinguishing between Norwegian and imported goods has to a greater extent been assigned to the *Godt Norsk* and *Nyt Norge* labels. The process of organising and 'cultivating' distinctive qualities had come far by this point. However, it remained somewhat unclear what were to be highlighted as the most important qualities for the Norwegian GI labelling scheme to promote. This was evident, for example, when the new scheme was described as *a sort of 'mini-version of Godt Norsk labelling' that should preferably be marketed together with the Godt Norsk label.* While qualities that have now become part of the Norwegian labelling scheme for PDO, PGI, and TSG formed a natural part of *Godt Norsk*, it is emphasised here that the scheme was seen as a sort of *mini-version of the Godt Norsk label.*

In addition to *translations, reorganisations* and *transformations* became important, and formed part of the plan for putting in place a scheme for origin labelling and the labelling of traditional foods. The emphasis on the need to *establish networks to cooperate on product development/adaptation* illustrates this. An awareness existed that actors must organise or reorganise themselves and cooperate to create new or transform existing products in accordance with a translated EU regulation.

The Standing Committee on Business and Industry submitted its comments on the white paper on Norwegian agriculture and food production in May 2000. In the summary of political focus areas, it is confirmed that *The Government also aims to establish a public system to protect distinctiveness and geographical indications for agricultural products and foodstuffs.* [22] It became clear in early June 2000 that the new Norwegian origin labelling scheme would form part of the Value Creation Programme for Food Production,[23] and the same document also mentions the motives for introducing the scheme.[24] The motives for introducing the labelling scheme are the most important thing to note from this section. It is pointed out that the scheme will:

- address consumer interests
- promote the development of quality products in Norwegian agriculture
- be a positive contribution to the development of speciality foods
- be an important basis for a value creation strategy

As part of the process of stepping up the adaptation work, a delegation from the Ministry of Agriculture went on a study trip to France from 27 to 30 June 2000. The programme was planned by industry attaché Einar Alme at the Norwegian Trade Council in Paris, and six members of staff from the Ministry of Agriculture took part. A report was written in connection with the study trip, and the preface refers to the trip being intended to strengthen the administrators' knowledge and translation competence in preparation for a scheme similar to AOC being established and adapted to the Norwegian context.[25]

At the time, it seemed like a natural and sensible choice to travel to France to study origin labelling, particularly in light of the country's long tradition of geographical indications. On the other hand, one can ask why France was chosen for this study trip instead of a country that it would be more natural to compare Norway to. The trip took place eight years after the EU's GI scheme was established. It would therefore have been easy to find a country that had already encountered challenges similar to those that would be faced in Norway.[26] AOC and the Norwegian GI scheme had very different preconditions for succeeding in the food cultures in which they were introduced, among other things because one was introduced on the initiative of the producers and traders, while the other was a political initiative. It is possible that part of the explanation for why France was chosen could be that the Norwegian quality turn has sometimes tended to romanticise the significance of labelling schemes and labelled products, and perhaps particularly their importance in Southern European countries and food cultures.

Although it has proven difficult to develop a Norwegian concept of terroir and to emulate other features of the Mediterranean food culture, the desire to 'become like France' has nevertheless played an important role in the quality turn to date. In the absence of this basis for comparison and trigger for adaptation work, the Norwegian GI scheme might never have been established. Had the romantic notion of cultivating a Norwegian food culture reminiscent of the idealised French culture not persisted, the adaptation work might even have broken down completely.

After seven years, it was stated that it was necessary to further tailor the Norwegian scheme for PDO, PGI, and TSG to suit Norwegian food culture.[27] In other words, the work of adapting the threefold European scheme to the Norwegian context was on the point of breaking down. Norway was not the first European country to face this challenge, however. This emerged in a green paper that was published in autumn 2008[28] and followed up in spring 2009.[29] The main conclusion was that the aim was still to have a scheme that protected geographical indications in the EU, but in a different form than had applied so far. This also reflects the adaptation work that was taking place in the EU because it was difficult to introduce a common set of rules in countries with different food cultures. The two examples from the Norwegian and EU public administrations show that adaptation work sometimes grinds to a halt or becomes impossible. Even if it sometimes comes to a halt, the adaptation work will continue, unless the scheme is discontinued. An adaptation breakdown can thus be understood as something that happens on different levels. Examples include a global system for GIs, the introduction of GIs in individual countries, and not least the adaptation breakdowns that producer organisations may experience during the application process. Despite these examples of adaptation breakdown, the comparison with France and other food cultures has been a crucial part of the adaptive force during the quality turn and the introduction of the Norwegian scheme for PDO, PGI, and TSG.

In June 2000, the action plan for Norwegian food culture (*Handlingsplan for norsk matkultur*) was published (Rusaanes and Hjortland). Like the study carried out under the auspices of the *Godt Norsk* foundation and the Norwegian Trade Council (NTC) and the Ministry of Agriculture's study trip to Paris, this action plan was developed on the Ministry's initiative. All these measures were important elements of the quality turn.

A proposal to amend the Act relating to Quality Control of Agricultural Products etc. in order to establish a legal basis for a Norwegian GI scheme was distributed to consultation bodies on 21 December 2000, with a deadline of 1 March 2011 for consultation submissions.[30] While this consultation process was under way, the Value Creation Programme for Food Production was launched on 3 January 2001. As mentioned above, the Competitive Strategies for Norwegian Food (KOSTRAT) were retained in this new programme. The Value Creation Programme for Food Production entails a further refining of terminology relating to product origin and geographical focus. The focus on the local/regional aspect points towards increasingly precise links to places (Value Creation Programme for Food Production 2001:10). Another interesting feature is that the term 'speciality foods' is highlighted (Value Creation Programme for Food Production 2001:4).

In their subsequent promotion of the Speciality label and the Norwegian scheme for PDO, PGI, and TSG, the Ministry and the Norwegian Food Branding Foundation (Matmerk) uses 'speciality foods' as a collective term for products covered by these two schemes. When innovation and the development of specialised foods are linked to Norwegian food traditions and local/regional speciality foods, it is natural to also interpret this as an implicit encouragement to transform already established products and develop new ones.

Organising the initiative to focus on the new qualities is a vital part of the quality turn. The focus on speciality foods is novel in itself and such an initiative also requires new forms of (re) organisation.

> Modern innovation theory attaches great importance to networks and cooperation as prerequisites for innovation activities. Mobilisation at the local community level is also considered important. A support scheme is proposed to encourage the establishment of *network organisations for primary producers*. The scheme should provide help at an early stage for producers that want to cooperate on developing and marketing quality foods aimed at markets with a high willingness to pay.[31]

This excerpt shows how financial adaptation was linked to organisation in the adaptation work that took place during the quality turn. Reorganisations are resource-intensive, and the authorities therefore propose granting financial support to promote cooperation, which will result in products based on the new qualities in the long term.

Adaptation challenges during the quality turn are in several places described as bottlenecks when identified in the 2001 report on the Value Creation Programme for Food Production.[32] In further adaptation work, we can see such bottlenecks becoming the subject of action plans, for example *Flaskehalser and etableringsbarrierer for mindre matbedrifter – en handlingsplan for å fremme nyskaping and få frem flere matbedrifter* ('Bottlenecks and barriers to entry for small food enterprises – an action plan to promote innovation and increase the number of food enterprises' – in Norwegian only) (Hjortland 2003). The report has a section dedicated to 'more knowledge about product protection – origin, tradition and speciality', which is typical of this phase of intensive adaptation work during the quality turn.

Action plans, in turn, give rise to concrete (re)organisation measures, for example *Tilsynsmodell for mindre matbedrifter – Prosjektrapport og Tilsynsveiledere* ('Official control model for small food enterprises – project report and control guides' – in Norwegian only) (Norwegian Food Safety Authority 2005).

> The project was initiated on the initiative of the Ministry of Agriculture and Food as early as 2003. The purpose of the project has been to arrive at a good model for guidance and supervisory work that will not entail unnecessary barriers for those who are engaged in or want to start up small-scale production of food.[33]

We see that this chain of adaptation work largely coincides with the introduction of the Norwegian scheme for PDO, PGI and TSG, and they both form part of the big picture of the quality turn. The introduction of fresh thinking on the issues of origin and new qualities triggers concrete adaptation processes, and the political process emphasises the organisational aspects of the adaptation work.

As shown above, the reorganisation of producers and producer collaboration are among the success factors emphasised at an early stage if the quality turn is to succeed. In 2010, (re)organisation continues to be a mantra for achieving the goal that has remained unchanged since the start of the quality turn. After ten years, it is still emphasised that primary producers must organise themselves differently in order to succeed.

The following steps can be important to ensure that projects increase the profit of primary producers:

• Ensure that the farmers act collectively. Primary producers must organise themselves in such a manner that their shared interest in retaining control over strategic advantages related to origin etc. is safeguarded by a relevant interest group. There are very few examples of individual farmers owning labels or identities in relation to consumers. It is difficult for individual farmers to safeguard their interests in relation to the sales chain and industry actors.[34]

The emphasis on and development of new forms of collaboration emerge as a key part of the adaptation work in the quality turn in general, and in the Norwegian scheme for PDO, PGI, and TSG in particular.

At this time, at the overarching political level, the development of the quality turn is visible in the past two government platforms. This comes in addition to the above-mentioned focus on organic production and consumption. The first Soria Moria Declaration stated that the government would stimulate the development of *niche products*.[35] The second Soria Moria Declaration stated that the government would stimulate increased investment in *speciality foods*.[36] Here, we note the shift from referring to products as niche products to speciality foods.

The authorities' work to define and their increasing use of the term 'speciality food' could be significant in different areas. Firstly, the definition of what constitutes a speciality food will be crucial to achieving the goals for the production and consumption of speciality foods in 2020. The development of an operational definition requires translation or a shift in the meaning of the term 'speciality food'. What is deemed to fall under the scope of the definition will, in turn, determine how soon the government can achieve its goal. The more products the definition applies to, the sooner the government will reach its goal.[37] Secondly, it could, for various reasons, be important for producers to be classified as producers of speciality foods. In such a case, a definition is a potential

point of departure for transforming products based on producers' wish to be included in the definition. This makes the mutual
relationship between the different adaptation practices clear. The
meaning of speciality foods is determined on the basis of actual
products, and actual products are transformed on the basis of the
definition of speciality foods.

In early April 2001, MPs Terje Johansen and Leif Inge
Kongshaug submitted a private member's motion to the Storting,
requesting the government to propose coordinating resources
from different Norwegian food culture programmes. The intention
was to strengthen Norway's food safety and develop competitive
Norwegian agricultural products with distinctive characteristics
and of high quality.[38] The motion was tabled during a relatively
active period of the quality turn. Coordinated organisation did
seem to be a relevant measure to propose. At this time, however,
too little time has passed to evaluate the separate effects over time
of the measures that had already been established. The motion
was not endorsed. A letter from the Minister of Agriculture dated
10 May 2001 was enclosed with the recommendation in which the
new labelling scheme for PDO, PGI, and TSG was highlighted.
The purpose of the letter was to refute the negative picture MPs
Johansen and Kongshaug had drawn of the organisation and
investment in Norwegian food culture when describing the background to their motion.[39]

It took ten years from when Johansen and Kongshaug tabled
their private member's motion for a dedicated development programme for speciality foods to be proposed and established in
2011.[40] During this period, the quality turn had progressed, among
other things through the Value Creation Programme for Food
Production. The new qualities stood more firmly on their own
feet. This made it easier to legitimise a continued focus on speciality foods than it was in 2001, when much of the adaptation and
quality refinement work remained to be done.

The producers' voice

When the Norwegian labelling scheme for PDO, PGI, and TSG
was prepared, the authorities largely took their inspiration from the
EU and Southern Europe. However, this does not mean that there
were no other influences. In addition to the formal consultation

rounds, Norwegian individuals, producer organisations and others influenced the development of the framework regulation through other channels, among other things because some of them were directly involved in the early adaptation work. Individuals and producer organisations involved in such work were able to exert influence during the process of drafting the framework regulation. The early involvement of producer organisations is an example of how adaptation work is relational in nature and reflects back on itself and future adaptations.

Another important factor was what bearing the understanding of the relationship between quality and place that the producer organisation in question had developed already by the mid-1990s, had on the development of the framework regulation for PDO, PGI, and TSG. As already mentioned, it may have seemed strategically useful to highlight a product and a place where this way of thinking already existed. At this time, and later as well, Valdres, Ringerike, and Røros were among the areas pointed out as regions where the relationship between products, people, and places was already an established trinity as regards the understanding of food quality. As I previously pointed out in relation to the choice of France as the destination for a study trip, it can in retrospect be questioned whether it was the right choice to primarily draw on knowledge from these Norwegian 'food preservation areas'. Using this strategy, the authorities endeavoured to cultivate a Norwegian way of thinking about quality and place, approximating as closely as possible what was believed to prevail in, e.g., France. The comparison between the 'food preservation areas', as representative of Norway as a whole, and France fuelled the further process and a hope that the scheme would be viable in Norway. On the other hand, it can be argued that highlighting these areas in the early stages of the process misrepresented the basis for establishing the scheme. In many ways, the comparison between Røros, Valdres, and Ringerike, on the one hand, and France, on the other, represents an exception in terms of awareness of the link between product and place, compared with Norway as a whole. In order to be better prepared for the subsequent food-cultural adaptation work, it would have been more natural to focus on the differences between the food culture in Norway and Southern Europe rather than emphasising exceptional cases from Norway that fitted the existing model. This approach would have raised awareness of the adaptation work that lay ahead – but in that case, the scheme might never have been introduced.

Establishing the Norwegian GI scheme

Proposition No 85 to the Odelsting (2000–2001) proposes amending the Act relating to Quality Control of Agricultural Products etc. to establish a legal basis for the framework regulation for the Norwegian GI scheme. The amendment was approved by the King in Council on the same date as the proposition is dated, 27 April 2001. Proposition No 85 to the Odelsting (2000–2001) and Report No 19 to the Storting (1999–2000) were the two most important and extensive documents in the preparatory works to the regulation. This is emphasised in an internal document from the Norwegian Food Safety Authority containing a list of documents for new case officers.[41] The amendment proposed in Proposition No 85 to the Odelsting (2000–2001) is also a concrete example of proposed rewriting as part of the adaptation work. The Norwegian Act relating to Quality Control of Agricultural Products etc. literally had to be rewritten to provide a basis in law for the new labelling scheme.

More or less immediately after the statutory amendment had been approved, the Ministry of Agriculture described the funding and division of responsibilities in the scheme as part of the annual agricultural settlement. This can be understood as the authorities' final report on the adaptation work carried out before the scheme was established.[42]

Following a period of increased focus on local, traditional, and niche products, it is again emphasised that the scheme will also apply to high-volume products. As mentioned, the scheme's establishment depended on a quality refinement process to identify the different product qualities on which it was to be based. However, this process broke down again at this time because of the intention for the Norwegian GI scheme to encompass both high-volume and local products.[43] This blending of different qualities is also evident in the use of the word 'tradition', which takes on an ambiguous meaning in this context. 'Tradition' is used to refer to agriculture in the sense of traditional cooperation or bulk production, but is also linked to the entity *Norwegian food traditions*. The blending of different qualities that occurred in connection with the introduction of the *Godt Norsk* label, where tradition and local aspects were included, re-emerged, but this time in reverse. When the Norwegian GI scheme was introduced, there was a wish to include high-volume production (implicitly at the national level). Of course, there are no clear-cut distinctions between these quality criteria, which also makes it difficult to cultivate them in complete isolation.

The examples of the blending of qualities in labelling schemes were part of the food-cultural adaptation work. *Godt Norsk* relies on tradition, and the Norwegian scheme for PDO, PGI, and TSG will benefit from including Norwegian high-volume products. The blending of qualities is also reflected in the ways in which the producers work, the shops sell products and the consumers consume them. Several of the producers who make products that are granted GI recognition, also produce high-volume products. The shops mix the specialities with generic products on their shelves. Consumers eat both specialities and cheap bulk foods. The labelling schemes are forced to be flexible to reflect the flexibility of the food culture.

Several documents relating to the Norwegian scheme for PDO, PGI, and TSG are dated 29 May 2001. I have previously mentioned that the motion for a coordinated Norwegian speciality food initiative submitted by Johansen and Kongshaug on this date was not endorsed. The Ministry of Agriculture described the funding of and division of responsibilities in the scheme in Proposition No 92 to the Storting, which is also dated 29 May 2001. There is also a third document in which the Standing Committee on Business and Industry submitted its recommendation regarding Proposition No 85 to the Odelsting (2000–2001) and endorsed the establishment of a new labelling scheme.[44] A letter was also enclosed from the Minister of Agriculture dated 18 May 2001 in which he responds to two questions from the Standing Committee on Business and Industry about the scheme's funding and how the labels are to be used and designed.

The recommendation from the Standing Committee on Business and Industry dated early June shows that the labelling scheme had already been taken into consideration as a policy instrument for value creation, despite not yet having been approved.[45] The recommendation shows that work continued on adapting products that could potentially be included in the scheme. It is difficult to say how far the adaptation work has progressed since 1996, when *Rakfisk*, *Gamalost*, and *Geitost* were launched as potential candidates. In this case, however, a geographical delimitation was introduced by the mention of the word *fjell* ('mountain'). A trend towards linking products more to specific geographical areas can be discerned.

The Standing Committee on Business and Industry's recommendation concerning Proposition No 85 to the Odelsting (2000–2001) was debated by the Odelsting on 7 June,[46] and the Committee's recommendation was unanimously endorsed.[47] The *Regulation on the Protection of Designations of Origin, Geographical Indications and Designations of Specific Traditional Character of Agricultural Foodstuffs* were adopted by the King in Council on 5 July 2002.

Predictions and trends

An op-ed article entitled 'Større mangfold av mat' ('Greater food diversity') was published in the Norwegian regional newspaper *Bergens Tidende* some months after the Norwegian GI scheme had been established in 2002. A clear note of optimism can be detected in the words of State Secretary Leif Inge Kongshaug from the Ministry of Agriculture:

> The Government's initiative will enable Norwegian agriculture to provide for and satisfy the growing demands of modern consumers in seven or eight years. Together, the new labelling scheme (the Norwegian scheme for PDO, PGI and TSG) and the Value Creation Programme for Food Production represent the first steps in this direction.[48]

A lot has happened since 2002, but the situation envisaged by Kongshaug in his article is still far off. Shortly after the labelling scheme's introduction, the goal was to have 20 protected products by 2007.[49] The aim was for these products to account for 1% of the total turnover in the Norwegian groceries market.[50] In 2005, the labelling scheme's strategic goal was still 20 product designations protected by law by 2007.[51] At an event held in Oslo Concert Hall on Tuesday 14 November 2006 to mark the scheme, Minister of Food and Agriculture Terje Riis-Johansen announced an adjusted goal for the Norwegian GI scheme. *The goal must be to have 20 designations and products with a sales value of more than NOK 1 billion by the end of 2008.*[52] During the event, *Gamalost frå Vik* was awarded the eleventh protected designation. However, the goal of 20 Norwegian products having been granted GI recognition had not been reached by the scheme's tenth anniversary.[53]

Some years after his predecessor's optimistic estimate of how many products would be approved by 2008, Minister of Agriculture Lars Peder Brekk made no secret of the fact that the authorities have been a driving force behind the quality turn: *I would go so far as to claim that the situation would probably have been very different without the Government's efforts to develop a policy for this field,* he writes in the op-ed article 'Lokal mat – nasjonale muligheter'.[54] Minister Brekk's emphasis on the role the authorities have played in the work of drawing attention and investment to what became a dedicated speciality food programme, is both correct and important. The development has not been characterised by a direct correlation between grassroot initiatives and the authorities' efforts in this area. The authorities have put a lot of effort into this, but it is nevertheless important to highlight concrete results that the authorities alone cannot take full credit for. New groups of producers and consumers have emerged over the past 20–30 years, such as farmers' markets, farm shops, local food shops, food festivals, restaurants, specialist shops and similar. All these examples can be regarded as consequences of the quality turn.[55]

A few years after his op-ed article in *Adresseavisen*, Lars Peder Brekk compared and balanced the 'new' trend against the volume strategy as follows:

Two lines of development: In this perspective, we can say that Norway's food supply policy and the food culture that we see today have been shaped by two lines of development.

1. Firstly, there is what we can call the volume strategy. This is a strategy for producing high-volume and standard products to ensure security of supply at the national level and a high and stable self-sufficiency rate. The overriding goals of this strategy are safe food, quality throughout the value chain, availability and competitive prices. This requires a competitive food industry.

2. The second strategy is what we can call the local food strategy, which is a regional development strategy to develop local foods with identity that are competitive in both the regional market and national sub-markets. In recent years, this strategy has produced many amazing products based on the regional natural conditions and distinctive food cultures. This has also contributed to regional business development, because food with distinctive local characteristics and identity is an important part of destination development in many locations. Food is increasingly considered an important part of the travel experience.[56]

This excerpt from the speech given by the Minister in connection with the celebration of the 20th anniversary of Fagforum for Mat and Drikke (Professional Forum for Food and Beverage) gives a more nuanced picture of developments over the past 20 to 30 years. The Clean Food strategy was an initiative in the late 1980s. It aimed to make Norwegian food more competitive at both the national and the international level. From 1992, the strategy was known as Competitive Strategies for Norwegian Food (KOSTRAT). In 2001, Competitive Strategies for Norwegian Food became part of the Value Creation Programme for Food Production, with an allocation of NOK 50 million in 2001. The Value Creation Programme continued until 2011. The 2010 national Agricultural Agreement allocated NOK 62 million to a development programme dedicated to speciality foods in 2011.[57] This allocation was partly based on the recommendations of a working group appointed to evaluate the Value Creation Programme for Food Production. The group concluded that a development programme dedicated to speciality foods from Norwegian agricultural producers should be developed as an extension of the Value Creation Programme.[58]

Looking back, this phase of preparations and introduction marked both an end and a beginning. It was the end of a consolidation phase of awareness-raising and defining the products and qualities to which the speciality foods category refers, and the beginning of concrete initiatives to promote this more or less established phenomenon. The Norwegian authorities have made targeted efforts to develop new and different food qualities. The Norwegian scheme for PDO, PGI, and TSG represents one of several food quality labelling schemes during the course of this development. A combination of industrial bulk and traditional small-scale production remains the status quo after the quality turn contributed to the crystallisation and nuancing of new food qualities and labelling schemes. However, the fact that the Norwegian scheme for PDO, PGI, and TSG has been developed and established does not mean that it is unambiguous, consensual and uncontroversial.

In sum

In this first sub-analysis, I have described how the initial ideas, preparatory works to and the establishment of the Norwegian scheme for PDO, PGI, and TSG formed part of the quality turn that emerged in Norwegian food policy and food culture from the late 1980s until the present day. The preparatory works to the Norwegian GI scheme were characterised by different and mixed motives related to key aspects of the quality turn. In line with the authorities' consumer orientation, it was argued that the scheme would benefit consumers. The Norwegian GI scheme was intended to give consumers a more diverse range of products and improve their access to information. In connection with the mobilisation against Norway becoming a member of the EU, it was argued that the scheme would also benefit producers. A third argument was that the scheme would help to preserve Norwegian food culture.

In addition to describing historical developments up until the scheme was established, I have analysed the introduction of the Norwegian GI scheme as an example of cultural adaptation work based on the elements such an approach comprises. Through this approach, I found that the most prominent cultural differences in connection with the introduction of the Norwegian scheme were linked to the significance of food and food quality and the social organisation of production, administration, sale, and consumption. Among other things, the new qualities that emerged during this period were imbued with meaning by being seen as a contrast to bulk products and comparable with products protected under the French AOC scheme. Politicians and the public administration were the most important actors in the adaptation work during this period, although producers and others also contributed. The introduction of the scheme required administrators to acquire knowledge about how the EU practised its GI scheme as well as how it could be translated to apply to Norwegian food culture. This helped to strengthen their adaptive competence. Overall, legal expertise was the most important knowledge during this period, but producers were also encouraged to put their tacit knowledge into words. Through adaptive competence, this knowledge was then used to adapt the scheme to Norwegian conditions. The most important adaptation practices during the preparatory phase of the Norwegian GI scheme were translation and reorganisation. Adaptation of meaning through translation is a recurring topic, both in the quality turn and in the translation of the GI scheme from a European to a Norwegian scheme. Reorganisation was also an important part of the work of developing an administrative model for the new qualities and the new scheme, which was adapted to Norway's food culture and the Norwegian context. Material transformations also occurred during this period. The activation and interaction between translations and reorganisations during the introduction of the Norwegian GI scheme formed part of the basis for future transformations. However, the transformations, especially of products, only became a central element during the subsequent administration and use of the scheme. The relationship between order and disorder is fundamental to the adaptation work. During the course of the quality turn, the adaptation work was intensified along the global/local and tradition/innovation dimensions. These dimensions were not particularly clear from the outset. However, they became increasingly relevant as endeavours intensified to develop the new food qualities and link them to international regulations for labelling schemes. The quality turn and the Norwegian GI scheme were primarily initiated by the authorities, a fact that also has a bearing on power relations. The introduction of the Norwegian scheme was largely controlled by the central government authorities. At the same time, it is clear that the new way of thinking about and understanding food and the GI scheme would not have been possible if it had been imposed from above without support at grassroots level. The inclusion of producers in the process of developing the Norwegian scheme is an example of how power shifts occur and form part of its adaptive force. However, the comparison with France was the crucial element in the adaptive force of the process during this period.

The importance of the focus on the national aspect, and on the national aspect as the basis for food quality, was greatest during the initial stage of the quality turn. The contextual framework expanded during this period, however. WTO, the EU, Norway, Røros etc. became important as geographical, contextual, and institutional levels. Other institutional contexts, of which politics, law and the economy can be said to have been the most prominent ones, were also important to the process.

The introduction of a new mentality as regards food by distinguishing and cultivating different food qualities is perhaps the most important result of the adaptation work carried out during this period. On the basis of the above, the development of food qualities can be described as follows: *Green and clean →National →Regional →Local.* Naturally, such a linear presentation does not show the whole picture. The new qualities emerge in the interplay between order and disorder. In this perspective, the adaptation work is one of the reasons why the Norwegian GI scheme was established since the scheme is based on precisely these new qualities. Another important reason why the scheme was implemented can be ascribed to the authorities' unrelenting insistence on comparing Norway's food culture and context, represented by Norwegian 'food preservation areas' such as Valdres, Ringerike, and Røros, with France. This comparison may have given decisive strength to the adaptation work. Without these qualities and the willingness to make comparisons, there would have been no basis or driving force for establishing a Norwegian GI scheme.

Extensive adaptation work had already taken place by the time the Norwegian GI scheme was established. However, equally important work lay ahead for all the parties that came to be involved in the scheme once it had been introduced. The following two sub-analyses deal with how food-cultural adaptation work continues to have a bearing on the subsequent administration and use of the labelling scheme.

Administration of the Norwegian GI scheme

Who would have thought that it was this complex? None of us thought so on the day we started on it, and I mean none of us. Neither in the Ministry or the Norwegian Food Safety Administration nor in Matmerk.[59]

Introduction

In this sub-analysis, I will deal with adaptation work in the administration of the scheme. The introduction of the Norwegian scheme for PDO, PGI, and TSG necessitated new administrative bodies and roles. The new food label also contributed to the reorganisation of existing administrative bodies that had to take the scheme into account in addition to their previously assigned duties. The three most important Norwegian administrative bodies and levels are currently the Norwegian Food Branding Foundation, the Norwegian Food Safety Authority, and the Ministry of Agriculture and Food. In an adaptation perspective, the national levels must also be understood in conjunction with the levels represented by EU and WTO regulations. Administering the scheme in accordance with both international regulations and Norway's food culture is an important and necessary task. The adaptation work carried out is reflected in the administration of the framework regulation and the application processes in particular. I will therefore devote particular attention to these two aspects of the scheme's administration. I will also shed light on other important aspects of the administration of the scheme that are characterised by adaptation work.

The data material differs significantly from the analysis of the preparations of the Norwegian GI scheme, as this sub-analysis is primarily based on interviews. I have supplemented these sources with other data where it was natural and necessary to do so. My aim is to show how the administration of the Norwegian GI scheme is characterised by cultural adaptation work.

The challenges administrators face in connection with reorganisations

The application processes are often lengthy – it is not uncommon for them to take several years. One of the administrators' main challenges during these periods is to get producers in the organisations to cooperate on the basis for and development of applications. The producers have to agree on many things. The tradition of being part of producer organisations with a common goal is often new, both to the administrative bodies and to the producers themselves. Some find it easy to cooperate, while it is more of a challenge for others. As I will elaborate on later, one of the producers I interviewed described the process of agreeing on a product regulation as having brought the producers together. This refers precisely to the transition from being organised as independent producers doing things in their own way to being part of an organisation and adapting to each other as a whole. The administrators in the Norwegian Food Branding Foundation witness and influence these reorganisations from the outside. One of them describes why it is often challenging and time-consuming for producers to reach agreement in the work towards the goal of GI recognition.

Administrator:	It is a long, drawn-out process. Not least for the producers to agree on what they are going to cooperate on.
AWH:	But why does it have to take so long?
Administrator:	Well, it doesn't really have to, I suppose. It depends on the groups we are working with. Some producers have strong family-owned constellations. They have each been kings of their own castle and have competed with each other. Obviously, for them to agree on which criteria to use, is a process, not least mentally. Suddenly, they are expected to cooperate in a way that they don't really have any tradition for. While, for others, cooperation comes more naturally.

The Norwegian Food Branding Foundation administrators see the actual organisation of the cooperation between producers as a major challenge. Reorganisation is demanding because they have to cooperate in a way that they have no tradition for. In addition to the reorganisation, the administrator also points out that they have to help the producers to mentally readjust. The producers have to think within the bounds of the regulatory framework that governs the Norwegian GI scheme, a framework that is based on quality being linked to the relationship between food, people, and place. They also have to learn to communicate their own know-how and traditions in a new way. The administrators face a two-fold challenge. Firstly, they have to get producers who have not previously worked together to cooperate. That requires reorganisation. Secondly, they have to help producers to mentally readjust, which requires them to translate the producers' know-how and the significance of the products.

The importance of knowledge and adaptive competence to the translation of product quality

In the administration of the Norwegian GI scheme, competence relates to being familiar with several food and knowledge cultures and having the ability to adapt them to each other. In order to adapt the EU regulations to Norwegian food culture and regulations, the administrators need knowledge about both. The same applies when producers have to adapt their tacit knowledge about cultivation and production traditions to the legal language used in regulations. In many application processes, this is not prior knowledge, but something that develops during the course of the adaptation work. In addition to knowledge about different cultures, adaptive competence also depends on a component that actually helps to adapt the different sets of knowledge to each other. The collective and individual adaptive force created around the phenomenon being adapted is such a component. As mentioned above, this is closely related to an understanding of and a desire to bring order to the different cultural components that initially appeared to be disordered. To put it polemically, it can be argued that the most important requirement for having a product protected under the Norwegian GI scheme has been omitted from the framework regulation. I refer to the willingness and ability to engage in food-cultural adaptation work, which is perhaps the most important condition that must be met in order to succeed with the work on the product regulations. The Norwegian Food Branding Foundation, producers, consultants, and others all contribute to this adaptation work. If the willingness and ability to engage in food-cultural adaptation work were no longer present, the whole labelling scheme would break down and no one would be able to achieve GI recognition.

The relationship between the different actors' knowledge and adaptive competence is brought into play when they endeavour to arrive at a shared understanding of what 'quality' means. The Norwegian Food Branding Foundation, local experimental societies, the research institute Bioforsk, the Norwegian Food Safety

Authority, producer organisations, consumers and consultation bodies all take part in this joint adaptation work, where the goal is to e.g. agree on what constitutes high quality for a specific variety of potato from a specific area.

The various actors' different knowledge comes into play and has to be adapted to each other. The producers adapt to the Norwegian Food Branding Foundation, the Norwegian Food Branding Foundation adapts to the Norwegian Food Safety Authority, the Norwegian Food Safety Authority adapts to scientific experts, and so on. This process goes back and forth, up and down between the different administrative levels. The actors participate in this collective adaptation work when they translate and assign a certain meaning to 'high quality', which then becomes a criterion in the product regulation, for example in the form of a percentage for dry matter content. This adaptation work depends on more than what the actors know about potatoes. Its success or otherwise is also determined by their ability, or competence, to translate their own knowledge about, e.g., quality or production methods into a set of regulations. Scientists, for example, have to translate their expert knowledge into specific quality requirements that are achievable for the producers. This differs from the adaptation required of producers, who have to translate their own, often tacit, practical and traditional know-how into descriptions of their production practices. In addition, the different actors must reach agreement between themselves. It is therefore important to the adaptation work to have insight into and knowledge of several cultures, as well as being a specialist in one. The best thing is to be a specialist in two fields at once and have the ability to unite them. Terms such as jack of all trades, renaissance person, polymath, bricoleur or *mångsysslare* (Ehn and Löfgren 2012:18) are used to refer to kindred spirits of these *adaptation workers*. They all master different fields or materials and put them into a context where the whole is greater than the sum of the parts. Together, they unite tradition with innovation and the local with the global – the *polytemporal* and the *polylocative*. Those who administer the Norwegian scheme for PDO, PGI, and TSG are precisely such competent adaptation workers when they introduce, administer, and adapt the Norwegian regulatory framework to those of the EU and the WTO, while also providing guidance to producers on how to comply with modern global rules as they apply for GI recognition of their traditional local products.

Translations and determination of the meaning of product quality have consequences for how the product organisations are organised and for the concrete products. Producers that already produce products that meet the criteria (e.g. dry matter content) defined by experts or the producers themselves, can more or less automatically become members of the producer organisation. Those who do not meet the criteria, are left out. One way of gaining entry to the producer organisation is to change the production method or the product to satisfy the translated requirements. Such cases involve different forms of adaptation work in that translations made by somebody – and of something – can trigger transformations and reorganisations in other actors and things. The balancing act between the EU model and the Norwegian model means that the administration of the Norwegian scheme for PDO, PGI, and TSG depends on knowledge, competence and chains of interacting adaptations.

Power shifts and adaptive force in the application process and between different actors

The adaptation work is characterised by different and shifting power relations. Weber's concept of *Macht* is suited to describing relationships between different administrative bodies and organisations. (*"Power" (Macht) is the probability that one actor within a social relationship will be in a position to carry out his own will despite resistance* (Weber 1978:53)). The parties are aware of the exercise of power involved and that some have a better chance than others of getting their way and having their arguments heard. The alternation between the different administrative bodies in the exercise of power helps the administration of the Norwegian GI scheme to progress and thus forms part of its adaptive force.

The excerpt below is an example of what can be described as guidance power. The interviewee is a representative of an administrative body who describes aspects of the perfect, from their point of view, application process.

AWH: How do you work together?

Administrator: When we receive an application?

AWH: Yes, and I would also like to know about what happens before that. Could you give a general description of the application process?

Administrator: They all differ a bit, depending on the actors involved. We think it's best when we come into contact with actors that are interested in the labelling scheme. Then we get the chance to provide guidance about what they have to work on, what they need to document and whether they really have any potential to be granted GI recognition.

Control of the framework conditions for translation, reorganisation and transformation in the application processes entails an element of power, but not such that it can be unambiguously associated with resistance and conflict. In the excerpt above, the administrator underlines the need for contact with actors that are interested in the labelling scheme at an early stage of the application process. This differs from a process where the actors operate on their own at first and contact the administrators once they have formed an understanding of the scheme and started work on the application. Guidance power is clearest in the early stages of a guidance relationship between administrators and producers, but it also exists at later stages of the application process. It fluctuates, depending on the producer's level of reflection and willingness to engage in dialogue with the administrators.

Adaptation work involves shifts in what knowledge is valid. Formally, the administrator's regulations-based knowledge outranks the users' tacit knowledge, but the producers' translation of their own practice and tradition is also very important when developing product regulations. The different kinds of knowledge are adapted to each other in a shifting power relationship. The administrators describe using different techniques and arguments while providing guidance to influence applications in the direction they consider best and most appropriate, given their understanding of the scheme's purpose. The framework regulation is nevertheless designed in such a way that the producers themselves decide which requirements are included in the different product regulations. The labelling scheme's importance to food diversity depends on the interplay and adaptation between the administrators' guidance power and the power producers have by virtue of being specialists in their own tradition and their own products.

Actors other than the administrators and producers also exercise power in the adaptation work related to the Norwegian GI scheme. Politicians, scientific experts, consumers, and retailers also form part of this 'power game'. They can all possess and exercise different forms and degrees of power. The grocery chains, for example, have a kind of chain power linked to e.g. logistics. It is important to many of the producer organisations to get their products on the shelves of the major supermarket chains. This means that they have to adapt to the chains' requirements. That is why the Norwegian Food Branding Foundation organises courses where producers can familiarise themselves with the systems, requirements and models of the chains.[60] Chain power is not necessarily considered a bad thing in relation to the Norwegian GI scheme, however. Producers can also benefit from it. Some producers say that the labelling scheme is important precisely because it gives them market access under agreements between the Norwegian Food Branding Foundation and the grocery chains. When the grocery chains focus more on speciality foods without relaxing their requirements, for example in terms of logistics, that could trigger transformations of both products and their packaging. In this way the chains play a part in the overall adaptation work relating to the Norwegian GI scheme.

As mentioned above, products that have already been granted GI recognition in the EU will 'automatically' be protected in Norway. This forms the basis for a broader discussion about adaptation power that also includes the relationship between Norway, the EU, and selected EU countries. While *Tørrfisk fra Lofoten* was the first Norwegian product to apply for protection under the EU's GI scheme, *Prosciutto di Parma* was the first EU product that applied for recognition under the Norwegian scheme for PDO, PGI, and TSG. The consultation letter describes how the Norwegian administration dealt with the application for the Italian product.[61] Among other things, the consultation letter deals with connections that can be interpreted as the relationship between adaptation work and model power (Bråten 2000). This combination of perspectives can yield insights into the power relationship between the translated Norwegian GI scheme and the EU's GI scheme. The consultation letter states that the conditions for protection in Norway are met for products that already meet the requirements of the EU scheme. This means that producers from the EU do not have to carry out reorganisations or transformations to be entitled to protection in the Norwegian market. The situation is different for Norwegian producers applying for protection in the European market. So far, they risk having to make adaptations despite having been recognised under the Norwegian scheme for PDO, PGI, and TSG. However, work is under way on an agreement for automatic EU approval of products approved under the Norwegian scheme. This asymmetrical situation can be interpreted as meaning that the original EU scheme has model power over the translated Norwegian system. Correspondingly, few questions are asked when a product granted a French AOC applies for approval under the joint European GI scheme (Barham 2003:131). In other words, a higher degree of adaptation seems to correlate with a lower degree of model power.

Despite this model power working in favour of France and the EU, it is important to emphasise that there are examples of translation work and model power going in the opposite direction. One such example is the acknowledgement that the Norwegian labelling scheme is an important tool in that Italian producer organisations actually apply for protection under it. In such cases, the adaptation work undertaken by the EU country in question consists of having the existing product regulation translated into Norwegian. This adaptation work is triggered because Norway is not a member of the EU, and because geographical indications are not included in the EEA Agreement. We can thus say that the Italian producer organisations adapt to the fact that Norway has chosen to remain outside the EU and that the scheme is not incorporated in the EEA Agreement.

Italian cheeses and Italian cheese producers formed the basis for the original Italian scheme dating back to 1954 (Rosati 2009:33). The Italian scheme was translated into a joint European system in 1992, and the Norwegian scheme established in 2002 was modelled on it. In 2010, several hundred years after the beginnings of Parmigiano Reggiano, the Italian producers applied to have their name protected in Norway. These examples illustrate the complexity of the relationship between adaptation work and model power.

As shown, the adaptation work is characterised by power shifts in more than one sense of the word. Firstly, there are shifts between different forms of power, but also between different parties exercising power and between different levels. At the same time, the power shifts contribute to adaptation dynamics, where people cooperate in a constructive manner towards a common goal. Cultural adaptation work thereby transcends conflict and harmony perspectives on cultural complexity and social change. Conflict and harmony are both part of the developmental dynamic in cultural adaptation work. Harmony and conflict are not seen as a point of departure or an outcome. The point of departure is adaptation, and the outcome is more adaptation, because increased adaptation also increases complexity. Power and adaptive force are important factors that complement each other in this dynamic and have a bearing on the direction of the adaptation work. Rather than being a negative manifestation of power in one or the other direction, adaptation work is a strategy for succeeding together.

The challenges administrators face in connection with their own and the producers' translations

When asked about challenges relating to adaptations made in connection with the introduction and administration of the Norwegian GI scheme, one of the administrators who played a key role in this work answered as follows:

AWH: What about implementing and using the EU regulation in Norway, is that difficult? Is there anything that is done in the EU that is impossible to do here?

Administrator (a): Yes, the names, geographical names. In the EU, it is a requirement that the name for which protection is applied must be a name that has traditionally been used for the product. An issue that we raised at a very early stage was that, if we are to apply the same assessment, then we might as well just put aside our work on this for a few years and tell the producers that they now have to start using the name that is linked to a geographical area, because we have no tradition for that in Norway. There is an incredibly small number of products that have been commonly referred to by a geographical name. Vossakorv sausage, Gudbrandsdalsost cheese, which is not produced in Gudbrandsdalen valley. Very few products have traditionally been linked to a geographical area. The traditional stew Trøndersodd has also been produced outside the Trøndelag region. There is Inderøysodd stew, but there are not many products. If we are to apply the same interpretation in Norway, that use of the geographical name must be traditional, because it is a require-ment that the designation must contain a geographical name, then we can just put our work on this aside for a few years, because that simply won't work here. Or we can say that we won't make it a requirement. It should be, the regulations say that the desig-nation must indicate the name of a region or a specific place.

AWH:	But there is no requirement that its use must be traditional?
Administrator (a):	No.
AWH:	While there is in the EU?
Administrator (a):	Yes, that's the interpretation that has been applied in the EU. At least, so we thought, until we learnt via the Ministry of Agriculture and Food that opinions differ among case officers in Brussels as well. Yes, it must have been used, but whether its use must be trad-itional, that we should require it to have been used for a long time, that was what there was some disagreement about.
Administrator (b):	But now it's been specified in the guide to the Norwegian regulations.
AWH:	So that's one of the things we have adapted here, simply because we don't have the same culture for it?

Administrator (a):   We just said that these are the facts. You can look at the EU's regulatory framework and interpret it in the same way, or you can say that, if this is to be a realistic strategy from 2002, then it must be interpreted differently.

While the producers' challenges are linked to the work on adaptation between the new Norwegian regulations and their own tradition, the administrators face additional challenges relating to adaptation work between the EU regulations and the administration of the Norwegian regulations. Producers and administrators are engaged in adaptation work between different levels or cultures. To put it simply, we can say that administrators work on adaptation between the EU and the Norwegian framework regulation, while the producers work at the interface between the Norwegian framework regulation and the product regulations.

One aspect that was translated for Norwegian food culture already in the first version of the framework regulation was that, initially, Norwegian food culture had virtually no notion of a relationship between product quality and origin. It therefore followed that there was no strong tradition of using place names to denote Norwegian products, while this is a requirement in the European GI scheme. This challenge was resolved by adapting the Norwegian regulations to *both* the EU *and* Norwegian food culture at the same time. Section 5 of the Norwegian framework regulation states that a designation of origin for a foodstuff may be protected provided that the designation indicates the name of a region or a specific place. This is modelled on the EU scheme, but, as mentioned above, the requirement is not compatible with Norwegian food culture, as few Norwegian product names are linked to a place. Section 5 was therefore adapted to Norwegian food culture through Section 6, which concerns exceptions from the conditions set out in Section 5. Section 6 states that a non-geographical name may be protected as a designation of origin for a foodstuff, provided that the name is traditionally associated with a specific region or place. The designations *Ringerikserter* and *Skjenning*, both of which have been granted PDO status, are examples of these different forms of association with a place. While *Ringerikserter* ('peas from Ringerike') meets the requirement for a geographical name set out in Section 5 of the Regulations, *Skjenning* does not indicate the name of a region or a place, and thus falls within the scope of Section 6. In the case of the traditional flatbread *Skjenning*, an assessment of what it means to be 'traditionally associated with' a region or place was decisive for the outcome of the application.

Naming and protecting products is a long-standing tradition in many countries. Laurence Bérard and Philippe Marchenay write that *French legislation has for many years endorsed the use of a geographical name to identify products whose characteristics are connected with a particular locality and know-how, and to prevent their imitation* (2008:13). In a food culture such as Norway's, however, it is part of the administrators' adaptation work to *create* a culture for using product names that are based on where they come from. In the course of the application process, the administrators will therefore ask some of the Norwegian producer organisations to develop names that link products to the place they come from. The possibility of adapting by adding the name of a geographical region to the designation, i.e. to construct a name, is also explicitly mentioned in the excerpt above. The example illustrates both the adaptation of the Norwegian regulations to the EU regulations and the adaptation of Norwegian food culture to the adapted regulations by adding a place to product names. The Norwegian scheme for PDO, PGI, and TSG thus contributes to the invention of a tradition (Hobsbawm 1983) for the relationship between product and product name, which is also a key feature of the quality turn in general. The fact that the Norwegian framework regulation is adapted to Norway's food culture does not mean that it is unproblematic for producers to comply with them, however. Firstly, few products have names that include a geographical name. The link has been erased or has been a blind spot in Norwegian food culture, and educational measures are required to see or remember it. The level of awareness of the relationship between food, people and places in Norwegian food culture can be seen as an example of the collective memory of societies and how they remember (Connerton 1989) – and forget (Connerton 2009). Also, as the administrator emphasised, it is of course difficult for producers to define what, to them, are self-evident connections.

Although the administrators' translation work can be challenging at times, help is available, for example through contact with the Portuguese Ministry of Agriculture, represented by the person in charge of Portugal's GI scheme. This person provides the Norwegian

Food Branding Foundation and case officers with information about how the European regulations are enforced and practised in Portugal. In the excerpt below, a staff member at the Norwegian Food Branding Foundation reflects on their own learning and adaptation to the EU/Portugal, and on how they draw on this knowledge in their dealings with producer organisations in Norway.

Administrator: We went to Portugal, probably four years ago, and went to visit producers that she had been working with for more than two years. And she said and repeated over and over: Yes, it was a type of rice, as I recall, 'yes, you are very good at describing that the rice is like this and the soil and climate like that, but why, then, are you unable to describe the link between them? That there is actually a link, or is there no link? Can that rice be produced in any sort of soil, or is that not actually the case?' And in some cases, the fact of the matter is that you can produce a product anywhere, it doesn't matter. And then you don't meet the criteria for a geographical indication. And some producers have that sort of product. They have a long tradition, strong roots in a geographical area, because they have worked and produced that product for many, many years, but they can't prove that it actually makes any difference that they produce it there. It's just tonnes of human know-how that has been accumulated. They are experts in the field because they've been doing it for over a hundred years, for example. But that's not enough.

The experience and knowledge about how Portugal deals with the joint European system are translated for use in the administration of the Norwegian scheme for PDO, PGI and TSG. The Norwegian scheme is thus modelled on the EU system in general, but also on Portugal in particular.

Another interesting point from the quote is the administrator's comment on producers being experts in their own product and their own tradition: 'They are experts, but that's not enough'. In adaptation work, it is, as I have already mentioned, preferable to both be an expert in one's own field and be able to translate one's expert knowledge within a different frame of reference. The case where a Norwegian producer organisation had to refute an expert soil survey report on a specific area can serve as an example of such challenges. In the report, scientists claimed that a certain product could not be grown in an area where this product had already been grown for generations and was still grown. While the scientists referred to soil samples and other scientific measurements to prove their argument, the producers referred to their own tradition and the fact that they had always grown the product in question there and were still doing so. In other words, the case involved not just one expert opinion, but several conflicting ones. The soil controversy ended with the research report being refuted through tradition, practice, and by certain misunderstandings being cleared up. This shows that while 'modelled on the EU' is the safest argument or the safest 'model' to adopt when discussing whether something is in accordance with the framework regulation or not, the actual production method is the strongest argument in adaptation work aimed at clarifying a production tradition.[62] The power shifts are thus linked to the force of the arguments, which can be based on science and on producers' practice. These examples bring us to the challenges relating to adaptation between laypeople, experts, and intermediaries.

Translations between laypeople, experts, and intermediaries

Successful adaptation work depends on the ability to take the other party's perspective. The experts must consider the problem from the layperson's point of view, and vice versa. It further complicates matters that administrators and producers alternate between the roles of expert and layperson in the adaptation work. The low opinion the one side has of the other side's knowledge of their own area of expertise is illustrated by the producers saying about an administrator that *he's never got his hands dirty*, or the administrators' descriptions of the producers, for example that *they have never had to describe such matters in writing*. While the administrators acquire most of their expert knowledge through formal education, the producers also possess practical know-how that is handed down from the generation before them. While the administrators are experts in rules and regulations, the producers are experts in production. Adaptation work occurs at the interface between the administrator's and the producer's translations.

In addition to the different starting points for adaptation represented by the administrators and producers, there is also an intermediary position, represented by consultants. Consultants often have a foot in both camps and can easily go back and forth between the actor positions represented by the administrators and producers. The consultants' adaptation work differs in nature from cases where the producers themselves have to adapt their knowledge to the legal format of the regulations or case officers have to understand the application from the producers' perspective. By transferring knowledge from one party to the other with relative ease, the consultant acts as a catalyst in the adaptation work. Ideally, consultants can communicate equally effortlessly with producers and administrators, but it is not a given that all consultants will be equally suited as adaptation workers.

The challenges administrators face when it comes to communication in connection with the administration of the Norwegian GI scheme can be understood in at least two different ways. Firstly, they are bound by their own specialised terminology. The administrative legal terminology and the requirements set out in the framework regulation must therefore be translated and adapted to the producers' knowledge, while the producers for their part try to familiarise themselves with the administrators' language. Secondly, the administrators find it difficult to communicate the requirements for PDO, PGI, and TSG to the producers, since the Norwegian food culture lacks the concepts needed to communicate the link between food, people, and places.

Administrator: We have tried to be more concrete and give examples when we write what we call a list of defects. As I said, we nearly always have to request additional documentation when we receive an application, so we call it a list of defects. There are defects in the application, and that sort of applies to everyone, because the regulations are complicated. In the early days, we tended to stick very closely to the regulations. We stuck to the practice and described it that way. That probably made for a very formal language that some producers would have found difficult to understand. When they received that letter from us, they thought: 'Oh my God, how can anyone write something so complicated?' So we have tried to work on our language, but at the same time we have to refer to the terms and provisions they have to comply with. But then we try to explain it more plainly. I'm not sure whether we are succeeding or not, but at least we've tried. But we have received feedback that the language in our lists of defects has been too formal and that producers have struggled to understand our letters. Some of them have struggled to understand what it is we're trying to say and what it is they need to do.

It makes for a difficult situation when a legal language that is not readily understandable to outsiders clashes with a working language that is not sufficiently developed to communicate the relationship between food, people, and places in the way the labelling scheme requires. This makes adaptation work a challenging endeavour that requires translations. It is when case officers and producers meet for mutual *ostensive learning* (Wittgenstein 2001:4) that this adaptation work is most effective. Those providing guidance make use of this form of learning in cases where they meet producers face to face. There is limited opportunity for ostensive learning in case processing, however. Once the application documents have been submitted to the Norwegian Food Branding Foundation, written language is the primary means of communication. The requirements in the list of defects are sometimes expressed and worded in such a way that it is difficult for the producer to understand what is required of them. The administrators try to adapt to the producers but find it challenging to translate legal terminology and content into a form that is understandable to others without losing the precision of the legal specialist terminology in the process. There is a difference between ostensive and document-based learning and communication. While the ostensive processes take place through face-to-face translations, the document-based ones are characterised by an objectification of meaning by turning it into documents in electronic or paper format that are moved between people in different locations.

The above excerpt emphasised the need for mutual understanding when developing product regulation. The parties need to communicate about how translations, reorganisations and transformations are to be practised in order to adapt to the regulations. The language is a tool in this adaptation work and is thereby one of the prerequisites for translations. At the same time, the language itself is being adapted and translated. A dual linguistic adaptation is taking place: when the working language is adapted, as described by the administrator in relation to the lists of defects, and also when producers translate their tradition into the legal language of regulations.

Consultation submissions that are received also bear the hall-mark of the jargon of the actors that submitted them. When the consultation submissions are collated by a legal adviser, the statements are translated into a language that can be understood as a language about the language. The legal language functions as a meta-language, or working language, in processes relating to the Norwegian scheme for PDO, PGI, and TSG. In the same way as the language of sociology is not immediately accessible to all, legal language is also a tool whose use requires some previous knowledge. If we turn the situation on its head, we find that the traditions that producers learn and pass down and their tacit knowledge can also be relatively inaccessible to the uninitiated.

The experts on both sides find it challenging to communicate with each other. This problem is sometimes resolved by employing a consultant who can adapt the producers' understanding to the language of the legal advisers and vice versa. One of the producers described the application process as difficult to relate to earlier in the interview. In the quote below, I ask the producer to elaborate on what it is that is difficult.

AWH: You said it was difficult to relate to …

Producer: I have to say that I read the regulations many times before I was able to grasp their substance. When I had read them a sufficient number of times, I called the Norwegian Food Branding Foundation. I plucked up the courage, you feel a certain awe … and perhaps you don't really speak the same language. Where we see a clear picture of our production premises and process, it is of course vague the other way. They don't know what it's about. They have received an application and

> have to respond to what is written in it. And we have
> problems communicating that this is something that
> has been a living process here from time immemorial.
> To us, it is so self-evident that we don't see the point of
> documenting it.

What is self-evident tacit and embodied knowledge to someone, is
difficult to communicate to others and for others to understand.
Knowledge that is taken for granted therefore presents a challenge
in the adaptation work. When what is self-evident to the public
administration encounters a producer organisation's self-evident
and unspoken knowledge, things are no longer so self-evident. The
differences between their knowledge about a local food tradition
and their ability to formulate it in the form of regulations become
obvious. The producer also indicates a certain feeling of awe in
relation to the administrators and refers to how this awe, or power,
is related to language, understanding, and being under guidance.
The early stages of the application process are often characterised
by such a sense of alienation.

Translation as an alienating and integrating practice

When producers are approaching the end of an application process and the product regulation is beginning to take shape, they
have made adaptations in several areas. Many find the early and
middle phase of the application process difficult, but nevertheless
perceive the adaptation and application work as a success once
the process has been completed. Such thoughts are expressed by
administrators when asked whether it is their impression that producers identify with the text that finally becomes their product
regulation.

AWH:	Do they identify with it?
Administrator (b):	It was they themselves who defined the tech-nical language, after all.
Administrator (a):	It is a result of the requirements in the appli-cation form. Take the description of the pro-duction method, for example. They write it down, right? It is done like this and this, the different parts of the production process, and

we incorporate that in the draft of the product regulation. And then, when they see it in black and white, when it has become a sort of requirement in the regulations, then there may be some parts that we need to cut because it is too detailed. But in the application form, they have to explain everything they actually do, so there is a bit of back-and-forth about what to include in the final version.

Administrator (b):   I don't think we have had a lot of feedback that the content of the product regulation is difficult to understand, because it is their own words.

AWH: You just enter them in the template?

Administrator (b):   Yes, we try to summarise, and pick bits from the application as best we can. Make it a bit more systematic. We have had feedback on our language sometimes, but not there.

Despite the administrators emphasising that the product regulation use the producers' own words, several informants – administrators, producers and consultants alike – suggest that producers feel alienated by the application process. It appears that the requirements for different forms and degrees of translation can trigger a sense of alienation. The shifts between distance and closeness between producers and their products that occur during the course of the application process can be understood as a three-stage process: First, producers know their own product and tradition, but a separation occurs when they have to deal with the labelling scheme. During the application process, their understanding of the production and their own knowledge is picked apart, so that they lose the sense of closeness and feel alienated. When the application process has progressed sufficiently, however, the closeness to the product is re-established, or producers experience a stronger integration with the product and their own tradition. The paradoxical aspect of this line of reasoning is that the wish to enhance consumers' sense of closeness to the products and the places they come from is sometimes pursued at the expense of the producers' own attachment to the products they produce.[63] In the attempt to make products less alien to consumers (Barham 2003:129), the producers are alienated in the application process. One of the producers described this as follows:

AWH: What does it feel like to have what has been a tradition here for so long put into legal language?

Producer: I don't know.

AWH: Can you identify with it?

Producer: Well, you do in the end, because then it has sort of been translated into our language, so to speak. Then it's really, then it's ours, then it's a formula that is sort of a product regulation formula, which goes section 1, 2, 3 and so on, that you have to stick to. Then there are the short things that go in there, and that's the important thing, and that is sort of fine.

Other producers have also stated that the legal language is hard to understand and must be translated back into their own language. However, the opposite of alienation can also be seen in the processes that unite producers in producer organisations. Some of these organisations were established for the purpose of achieving a geographical indication. In such cases, a fellowship that did not previously exist arises around the products. Some also seem to feel an even stronger attachment to the product and tradition once the product has been finally approved and its name granted protection.

Reorganised impartiality and legitimation work

The Norwegian Food Branding Foundation, the Norwegian Food Safety Authority and the Ministry of Agriculture and Food all organise their work related to the Norwegian scheme for PDO, PGI, and TSG in such a way as to ensure impartiality. In the Norwegian Food Branding Foundation and the Ministry, the functions are divided between staff who work on business development and staff with formal legal responsibility for the scheme. The Norwegian Food Safety Authority's functions are divided between the regulations department and the control department. The Norwegian Food Branding Foundation's specialist department undertakes the formal case processing, while other staff provide guidance to producers in connection with their work on applications. The rationale for separating these functions is linked to a requirement and wish for impartiality. A similar emphasis and division of tasks are found in the Norwegian Food Safety Authority. The organisational changes in connection with the reorganisation of the Norwegian Food Safety Authority in 2007 also had a bearing on the division of administrative responsibilities. While the control department ensures that products comply with the regulations, the regulations department ensures that the regulatory development produces regulations that are both suited to Norwegian food culture and modelled on the EU system. We can therefore say that the control department and the regulations department influence and engage in different types of adaptation work. The control department concerns itself with the relationship between transformations and translations, while the regulations department focuses on the relationship between different translations. This division of responsibilities was in turn a result of reorganisation work. The Norwegian GI scheme thus both gives rise to and is influenced by reorganisations in other areas and institutions.

There appear to be clear internal dividing lines between the administrators tasked with promoting use of the scheme and those who process applications in both the Norwegian Food Branding Foundation and the Ministry of Agriculture and Food. Although it strengthens impartiality, this division of roles and responsibilities is sometimes perceived as a complicating factor, both by applicants and by the administrators themselves. The Ministry issues guidelines for the Norwegian Food Safety Authority, which is in turn charged with assessing the administration of the Norwegian scheme for PDO, PGI and TSG in light of the reorganisation of the Norwegian Food Branding Foundation. Overall, the adaptation work in relation to impartiality management is intended to maintain the boundaries between what can be adapted and what should not be mixed. The Ministry and the Norwegian Food Branding Foundation are organised to avoid mixing purely legal issues with activities intended to promote business development. The Norwegian Food Safety Authority is organised to keep regulatory matters separate from supervisory practice.

Revisions of the framework regulation

The framework regulation for the Norwegian scheme for PDO, PGI, and TSG were revised seven times between its introduction in 2002 and year-end 2011.[64] These amendments are interesting and concrete examples of how administrators initiate and implement food-cultural adaptation work by adapting the regulation to Norwegian food culture, organisational changes, other regulations and the European GI scheme. The further development of the regulation did not come out of the blue. The inclusion of fish and a general expansion of the range of products covered were both mentioned already in the preparatory works to the regulations.[65]

We find the first interesting and simple example of how regulations are translated in the discourse on the Norwegian scheme for PDO, PGI, and TSG.[66] The term 'framework regulation' is often used in this discourse, although, as the administrators mention, this term does not seem to be used in Norwegian legal terminology. The term is probably a variant and an approximation used as an adaptation and translation of a concept from the terminology used in the EU. Despite the fact that the regulation governing the Norwegian scheme for PDO, PGI, and TSG are not, formally speaking, framework regulation, this term has been retained in the work on translating the scheme. The phrase 'framework regulation' has been repeated so often in the discourse about the Norwegian scheme that it has come to sound as natural as 'modelled on the EU' – and the phrase 'framework regulation' is perhaps a very good example of precisely that. The Norwegian specialist legal terminology is enriched, or colonised, by the EU terminology to enable changes to be made to the Norwegian regulatory framework and food culture.[67] We can thus say that two forms of adaptation work together at this level. The adaptation of Norwegian food culture results in legal adaptation in the form of direct translations.

The continuous adaptation work at framework regulation level in relation to the EU and Norwegian food culture in general will have consequences for individual applicants, who depend on being up to date on regulatory developments when submitting an application for consideration. The consultants also express frustration about the fact that things are constantly being adapted and take time.

Guidance can be beneficial as regards keeping up to date, according to some producers and consultants. An application process under guidance makes it easier for applicants to keep up to date with the complex and sometimes adjusted regulatory framework they have to navigate.

Table 2.1 The adaptation practices and consequences of revisions of the framework regulation

Entry into force	Adaptation to	Adaptation practice	Most important consequence
5 July 2002	European and Norwegian food culture and regulatory framework	Translations, reorganisations	Establishing a scheme for protecting product designations
24 October 2003	Norwegian and Italian food culture, as well as the Norwegian regulatory framework	Translates the significance of fish in Norwegian food culture to also apply to the scheme	The scheme's product range expanded to include fish
13 February 2004	Organisation of the Norwegian public administration	Translates the reorganisation from the Norwegian Food Control Authority to the Norwegian Food Safety Authority into the regulations	A new administrative structure for the scheme
19 March 2007	Norwegian food culture	Translates the regulation to apply to foodstuffs in general	More or less all kinds of food are covered by the scheme
18 May 2007	EU law	The requirement for *reputation* is removed to increase similarity to the European scheme. An incorrect translation is corrected.	The regulatory conditions are made stricter
1 January 2010	Fee increase	Pricing[96]	The price level of application fees maintained
17 December 2010	Fee increase	Pricing	The price level of application fees maintained
19 December 2011	Fee increase	Pricing	The price level of application fees maintained

The review of the seven revisions of the framework regulation specifies and provides a picture of the administrators' adaptation work. Without going into the details of every amendment in every revision, it also clearly illustrates that adaptation work is taking place that can be understood from different adaptation practice perspectives. To summarise, we can say that revisions of the framework regulation fall under the adaptation practice of *translation*, which has organisational, material and financial consequences. The revisions are summarised in Table 2.1.

The amendments to the framework regulation bear concrete witness to how the food-cultural adaptation work functions in the administration of the Norwegian scheme for PDO, PGI, and TSG. They show how the new labelling scheme influences Norwegian food culture modelled on the EU, but also how the food culture and other factors influence the scheme. The revisions of the framework regulation also show that the adaptation practices themselves are adapted to each other when activated to adapt cultural differences across different levels.

Modelled on, modelled on, modelled on …

The phrase 'modelled on the EU' is almost a mantra in the Norwegian discourse on geographical indications. The interweaving and adaption of different models feature more prominently in the actual adaptation work, however. Adaptations are modelled on Røros one day and on the EU the next day. One day, the emphasis is on smoking meat in traditional timber saunas, the next day the topic under discussion is drying meat in climate-controlled chambers.

The excerpt below refers to the relationship between levels of translation that can also be said to represent different patterns or models. The interviewees are consultants discussing adaptation work from their intermediary position between the administrative body and the producers.

Consultant (a):   First, we had a round with the Norwegian Food Branding Foundation, essentially to gain an understanding of how things were supposed to be. And then we have to transfer that to the working group, and then we add our interpretations to the mix, you see? And

	as a result of our interpretations maybe not being quite correct sometimes, and not maybe being in agreement with the Norwegian Food Branding Foundation, the Norwegian Food Branding Foundation became involved on several occasions to resolve the issues. So the working group also had direct feedback from the Norwegian Food Branding Foundation. That resolved a lot of the discussion about traceability, for example. Where people have understood that there is actually a job to be done here to succeed in getting the geographical indication.
AWH:	So there has been direct contact with the Norwegian Food Branding Foundation when you were working, they have been part of the working group?
Consultant (a&b):	No, yes, sometimes.
Consultant (b):	Yes, they've given talks ... Explained the scheme a little.
AWH:	What was the reaction like the first time they attended the working group after the meeting at which they presented the scheme?
Consultant (b):	I think they found it really positive. In a way, they got to hear a little more and learned more and, not least, understood more. I think it was really positive and helped us a lot, so it was really good.
Consultant (a):	Yes, because we did have some important discussions in that setting ...
Consultant (b):	They could put questions to them directly that were not about our application, but were also a bit more general.
AWH:	About the regulations in general?
Consultant (b):	Yes, the scheme.

The above excerpt makes it clear that many actors, levels and models are involved in the adaptation work. The producers have established a working group consisting of consultants and representatives of the producer organisations. The consultants state that they take active part in the translation work, and that they sometimes realise their own limitations. In this case, they asked the Norwegian Food Branding Foundation to explain the scheme directly to the producers. This example of calibration of the understanding of the labelling scheme takes the producers and products as the point of departure and moves towards a general level. Another approach is to take the general level as the point of departure. The organisation and governance of the public administration and policies relating to the Norwegian scheme for PDO, PGI, and TSG can be understood from such a perspective. This is in line with the form of governance referred to by Lie and Veggeland as *multilevel governance* (Lie and Veggeland 2010:11). Lie and Veggeland point out that a new form of problem-solving develops in parallel with multilevel governance, which entails the local, national, European, and global levels becoming more closely intertwined. Lie and Veggeland do not explicitly mention 'adaptations' but emphasise the different actors' decisions and decision-making competence. However, the adaptation work between different levels and actors is at least as important an aspect of decision-making as the actual decisions that are made. The different levels and actors adapt to each other, something that Lie and Veggeland touch on when they point out that the different levels influence each other both upwards and downwards in the multilevel system. In this perspective, competence is not only important in relation to decision-*making* at one governance level. The ability to *adapt* preparatory works for decisions between these levels is at least as important. In addition to the focus on formal decision-making levels, it is also important to emphasise that various actors influence the food-cultural adaptation work – including actors that are not part of a formalised food policy or administrative decision-making level. For example, the extent to which a producer organisation adapts to the framework regulation will have consequences for whether the application is granted by the Norwegian Food Branding Foundation and the Norwegian Food Safety Administration or whether it is decided at the ministry level, as in the *Ringerikspotet* case, or at the European level, as in the case of stockfish, or whether the decision goes all the way to the WTO level, as in the discussions concerning the possibility of global regulations for geographical indications for foodstuffs modelled on the existing system for wines and spirits. The regulatory levels thus constitute clear levels and models in the adaptation work. While the TRIPS Agreement defines guidelines for the EU, the Norwegian GI scheme is modelled on the European scheme. The framework regulation set out national guidelines, while the local element is manifested in the product regulations. The specific know-how, practice-related and material circumstances relating to production and consumption that the product regulations regulate can be said to represent concrete aspects of food culture at a local level. The levels and models range from the most general phrase in the TRIPS Agreement and the adaptation of the EU's regulatory framework to accommodate requirements from the USA and Australia, to, for example, the requirement that *Gamalost frå Vik i Sogn* must be ripened using the mould *Mucor mucedo* and that the mycelia that develop during the ripening process must twice be patted down into the cheese by hand to encourage it to grow inwards.[68]

The Chinese puzzle box is frequently used as a metaphor for the relationship between different levels. This image can be interpreted as the local aspect forming an inner core of the global (the box on the left). When also talking about the global in the local, it is necessary to demonstrate that the figure works just as well when turned inside-out (the box on the right). These two ways of understanding the scheme can be understood as a global top-down (left) and a local bottom-up (right) perspective on studies of the Norwegian GI scheme.

The perspective from which each actor perceives and understands the regulatory framework depends on their point of departure. The choice of perspective will therefore have a bearing on the choice of

Figure 2.1 Global and local perspectives on geographical indications.

method and theory. The ideal approach, however, is to combine these perspectives and explore adaptations between the different levels and the relationship between them. This relationship and the links between regulatory levels give rise to a need for adaptation work. The food cultures of which the regulations form part are nevertheless crucial to the adaptation work taking place.

The regulatory levels represent different models for patterns of action that are continuously adapting to each other. There are thus a variety of models for how GI schemes are applied. Different countries and food cultures choose models that they create and adapt: the EU models its scheme on France, Norway models itself on the EU and Røros, WTO models itself on the USA and the EU, and so on. One day, the focus is on one's own food culture, the next day on the French AOC scheme. The Norwegian scheme for PDO, PGI, and TSG is continuously evolving under the influence of other GI schemes. Taken together, this all comprises the global cultural adaptation work on food cultures and regulatory frameworks.

In sum

In this sub-analysis, I have described the administration of the Norwegian scheme for PDO, PDI and TSG and how it is characterised by adaptation work. I have demonstrated the significance of the different administrative adaptation practices separately, as well as how they interact with each other and can be understood as chains of adaptations. The administrators' descriptions of their work both correspond to and differ from the story told by the representatives of producer organisations. They are similar in that both groups point to challenges when it comes to getting the scheme to accord with Norwegian regulations and Norwegian food culture. The stories differ in that administrators and applicants describe different roles in the adaptation work. Since administrators have a different remit, they naturally see other challenges than the applicants do. They see it as a challenge to get producers to organise themselves in new ways. They see it as a challenge to get producers to think about their products in a different way and to translate their knowledge into a product regulation. They see it as a challenge to model the Norwegian scheme for PDO, PGI, and TSG on the EU, while also ensuring that it works in Norway.

In addition to describing the different aspects of the administration of the scheme, I have analysed the administration in the context of cultural adaptation work and the elements that constitute such an approach. Through this approach, I found that the most prominent cultural differences associated with administration are linked to meaning and organisation. Examples include work on defining what is meant by product quality and how the administrative bodies are organised to ensure impartiality in their adaptation work. The administration's definitions and power over meaning also have a bearing on the producers' transformations. The most prominent actors in the administration of the Norwegian GI scheme are administrators, producers, and consultants, and the relationships between these actors are important. Many other actors also form part of this picture. It is clear in relation to the administration, as it was in connection with the introduction, that the actors the scheme concerns are themselves co-constructors of the labelling scheme. The administration takes place in an interplay between different actors' adaptive practices, largely centred on the administrators' legal knowledge. Nevertheless, the administration of the scheme requires knowledge about how the GI scheme is practised in the EU, and about how it can be translated to fit Norwegian food culture. When the administration's self-evident knowledge encounters the self-evident, tacit knowledge of a producer organisation, a need arises for adaptation work and the competence required to carry out such work. Translations, reorganisations and transformations are all important adaptation practices in the administration context. While translations and reorganisations appear to be the most important elements and are carried out by and with the administrators themselves, transformations appear to be an outcome of the administration work and something that is largely practised by the producers. Basically, the adaptation work takes place along the order/disorder dimension, as well as the global/local and tradition/innovation dimensions. Several forms of power are in play. I have shown how the administration entails different forms of *Macht*, guidance power and model power. The power dynamics between different administrative bodies and other actors help to ensure that the administration of the Norwegian GI scheme progresses. The administration of the Norwegian scheme is part of the quality turn and must be understood in light of this process and other contextual conditions, including different institutions where science, law and financial considerations can be said to play a particularly prominent role. As I have already mentioned, the collective and individual adaptive force created around the Norwegian GI scheme is linked to an understanding of and wish to bring order to what initially appeared to be disordered.

The adaptation work in the administration of the Norwegian GI scheme has several important consequences. Firstly, the scheme is adapted to conditions in the EU as well as in Norway. It can be shaped to fit Norway's food culture, but the food culture is adapting to the scheme at the same time. Concrete examples include amendments to the framework regulation and the development of product regulations. The development of these two types of regulations is also an arena where shifting power relationships between different actors are played out, contributing to the GI scheme's development and adaptation. However, another consequence of the continuous adaptation work is that it may be difficult to keep up to date with current practices in the EU and in Norway. The development of product regulations also results in producers, through translations and reorganisations, alternating between a sense of alienation from and closeness to their own products and other producers. Furthermore, the final product regulations mean that some producers are allowed to call their products by a certain name, while others are excluded. Overall, the adaptation work carried out by administrators plays a role in deciding how producers understand their own products, production and tradition. It also influences the producers' organisations and the material characteristics of the products. The adaptation work that is part of the Norwegian GI scheme's administration thus has a bearing on the development of Norwegian food culture, alternating between standardising and diversifying it.

The use of geographical indications in Norway

We have pooled the knowledge we have inherited, all of us, and reached an agreement on how to describe it. Then we have received feedback from the Norwegian Food Safety Authority, via the Norwegian Food Branding Foundation, that it wasn't good, but now it's okay, and then we accept that. Then we have a draft of our product regulation.[69]

Introduction

Different actors use geographical indications in different ways and for different purposes. Among other things, the Norwegian GI scheme is used as an agricultural policy tool, grocery chains use it for marketing purposes, and consumers use it to make informed decisions about which products to buy. In this sub-analysis, I primarily concentrate on how producers use the scheme by focusing on their work on applications.

Producers must comply with the conditions set out in the framework regulation when submitting an application. These conditions thus form the point of departure for various types of adaptation work, depending on what the conditions concern. Some producers take a long time to decide who will be included in the producer organisation, while other spend a lot of time developing the product name. In some cases, neither the organisation nor the product name existed before the adaptation work began. In these cases, both must be established and adapted during the course of the work. Some producers find the application process for a geographical indication a positive experience. Among other things, they point to the process being educational and having an integrating effect. Others find it a negative experience, for example if the application process was unclear and difficult to complete successfully.

I have already shown that the adaptation work associated with the preparations and administration of the Norwegian GI scheme is characterised by *reorganisations* and *translations*. The producers' use of the scheme also includes *transformations* as a key adaptation practice. Producers adapt to each other and adapt their way of thinking, and they also transform their products and other material factors in accordance with the collective requirements set out in the product regulations. Like translations and reorganisations, the extent of the transformation work also varies between producers.

In order to shed light on the diversity of adaptations involved in the Norwegian GI scheme's use, I have chosen to organise this final sub-analysis around the most important conditions and requirements that must be fulfilled in order to be granted GI recognition. I will begin with the preparatory works to the regulations (Proposition No 85 to the Odelsting (2000–2001)) and Section 14 of the framework regulation. They set out conditions related to *quality* and *form of organisation*, respectively. I will then largely focus on Section 9 of the framework regulation. This section contains a seven-point list specifying the required content of applications for PDO and PGI. The reason why I choose to omit TSG from this context is that I have fewer data about this form of protection and that the requirements that apply to TSG, set out in Section 12 of the framework regulation, are largely identical to those that apply to PDO and PGI status.

The sub-analysis is mainly based on interviews with producers and consultants, but I have also used other material as a supplement where I have found it natural and necessary to do so. Overall, I will show how use of the Norwegian GI scheme is characterised by and relies on cultural adaptation work.

Formalisation and reorganisation of producer organisations

Any organisation may apply for regulation (product regulation) to be adopted for the protection of a designation of origin, a geographical indication or a designation of specific traditional character.[70]

There are several possible approaches to studying how producer organisations are formed and further develop their products within the framework of a geographical indication. One possibility is to focus on 'success stories' and emphasise how joining forces help producers to increase their market share and safeguard the quality of their product (Canãda and Vázquez 2005). In this analysis, however, I focus more on the *challenges* producers face in the adaptation work required to become a consolidated group.

It varies how challenging it is to clarify who is to be included as a member of a producer organisation. Sometimes, it is easy because there is already a fairly established group. In these cases, the producers usually come from the same place and produce quite similar products in similar ways before they decide to apply. Another example is when a few applicants decide to form an organisation. In cases such as these, it is often only a question of formalising a pre-existing form of organisation. At other times, the initiative comes from producers that have not been part of a group, or an organisation can be a result of an outside initiative. In these cases, there is work to be done to create or reorganise a producer organisation that did not have concrete plans to apply for a geographical indication. The producers then have to work out which producers should be included in the organisation. Consultants are sometimes also asked to put together a group of producers for cooperation purposes. The excerpt below is from an interview in which two consultants share their experience of such an assignment.

Consultant (a):   We sent a query asking whether anybody wanted to join.

AWH: Because you have a pretty good overview of the producers of this product?

Consultant (a):   Yes, we had done some preparations first and sent information to all relevant enterprises. Then we received feedback from them. Those that said yes were the potential members. Then we asked if any of them wanted to take part in a working group. We reserved the right to decide the composition of the working group to a certain extent, to ensure that there would be a balance between big and small producers, and things like that. Then we were left with the ones who were committed to the process and who wanted to work on it.

AWH: Was there broad support?

Consultant (b):   No, not really. It was the ones we expected. We know them pretty well.

The above quotation highlights certain aspects of the consultants' expertise. They have knowledge about the product, know the producers and have little difficulty identifying which producers should be members of the organisation. In this case, the adaptation work entailed both formation and reorganisation: formation in the sense that the organisation represents a newly formed social and financial constellation, and reorganisation in the sense that producers organise an established form of production in a new way in cooperation with others.

There is always someone who takes the initiative as regards who will cooperate on submitting an application and developing product regulation. However, it is not until the regulations exist, with requirements regarding geographical area, production method and product qualities, that it is formally delimited who can participate. Such delimitations exclude some producers and products, but the work of agreeing on product regulations also creates a stronger sense of fellowship in relation to the products. When asked how the cooperation in one of the producer groups has functioned, one of the producers answered as follows:

Producer: It has been brilliant. I am very impressed by how the process has brought us together. Over the past year, we've worked very closely with each other. Worked our way through the regulations with the Norwegian Food Branding Foundation.

Later in the same interview, we touched on the uncertainties associated with applying for a protected geographic indication and the consequences if the application is rejected.

Producer: We have also discussed the possibility of not being granted a geographic indication. No, that doesn't really matter. We've done a great job, we think, no matter the outcome. Because now we are a close-knit bunch who will cooperate in future, even if we don't succeed this time. I do realise now, in this process, that it's not as easy as it seems. We could actually risk being turned down.

The producer describes how their cooperation on learning and thinking in a certain way, while agreeing on what the products should be, has had an effect on the group. The adaptation work has turned a group of people who used to work on their own into a close-knit bunch. The individual producers have become part of a group. This integrating effect means that the reorganisation is regarded as a success regardless of whether or not they succeed in achieving GI recognition.

Different administrator roles in the Norwegian Food Branding Foundation are separated by organisational boundaries. The Norwegian Food Branding Foundation administrators who work on the legal aspects of the scheme state that the conditions set out in the framework conditions are so complex that neither consumers and applicants nor other the Norwegian Food Branding Foundation staff are capable of distinguishing between the different geographical indications. The Norwegian Food Branding Foundation's organisational boundaries between the case processing and guidance roles are intended to ensure order and impartiality. The division of roles is nevertheless perceived as challenging in relation to the adaptation work that is carried out.

At the initial level of adaptation work, producers and administrators represent different knowledge cultures that have to be adapted to each other. The quotes above show that the situation is more nuanced, however. At a second level, internal reorganisations also take place between producers and between administrators. The producers in the producer organisations adapt to each other in relation to geographical affiliations, production traditions and product qualities through, and as a result of, reorganisation. The Norwegian Food Branding Foundation's staff also include people with backgrounds from different professional traditions. They understand the regulations from their point of view and their knowledge, which, in turn, have to be adapted to other Norwegian Food Branding Foundation staff and applicants. Reorganisations are intended to bring order to the internal situation in the organisations and the administration, but also to the relationship between them. A number of challenges nonetheless arise in connection with such organisation and reorganisation processes. Like the administrators, consultants also find this adaptation work challenging.

One consultant mentioned that not all Norwegian Food Branding Foundation staff have the same understanding of the Norwegian GI scheme, and that this has had an impact on the application process. When the consultant mentions that they have also had an impact on the Norwegian Food Branding Foundation's administration, that is no coincidence, however. Unlike the administrators and producers, consultants have a dual horizon of understanding and, ideally, also the ability to expand the administrators' and producers' understanding of each other by translating and adapting the exchange of opinions between them. In this interaction, the consultant helps producers and administrators to alternate in their communication between being the sender and the receiver of each other's knowledge. The consultant can thereby contribute to organisational adaptations in producer organisations, and internally within the

Norwegian Food Branding Foundation, in order to impose order at the product, production and administration level. When such reorganisations take place, they also radically change the systems of meaning that were already established before the adaptation of the social relations. This shows how reorganisations and translations are related. Changes in social relations produce changes in how a phenomenon is understood. The producers develop a different understanding of their own products and tradition when they become part of new producer organisations and have to translate their production practice into a language that other producers and the administrators can understand. We see the same in the Norwegian Food Branding Foundation when administrators from different backgrounds understand the Norwegian GI scheme in different ways and have to adapt to each other's understanding. Such reorganisations take place because Norway's food culture has not had a strong tradition for this type of cooperation between producers, consultants and the public administration.

Reorganisations also relates to how producers ensure the high quality of their products. One way of doing this is to sort out what they already have a tradition for producing based on the reorganised organisation's translation of the production tradition into conditions for high quality in the product regulation.

Sorting out high quality

As part of the value creation strategy, the labelling scheme will therefore emphasise stimulating the development of speciality foods of high quality based on Norwegian food traditions, as well as local and regional specialities, and where other countries can have served as inspiration.[71]

The question of product quality is a key topic in studies of the Norwegian scheme for PDO, PGI, and TSG. Quality understanding is mentioned as a natural part of 'the quality turn'. It refers to producers and consumers' turn towards other forms of product qualities than those associated with industrial production (Goodman 2004). Another important approach to the quality aspect relates to standards of hygiene (Muchnik et al. 2005). There is also a focus on how the understanding of quality varies between different cultures that have introduced such schemes. Such studies discuss quality based on the divide between Northern and Southern Europe (Parrott et al. 2002). A fourth approach to the concept of quality is how product qualification is geared to a quality standard and what effect this has on producers and the local community (Tregear et al. 2007). All these and other perspectives on quality include different forms of quality adaptations.

Like in the European scheme, the preparatory works to the Norwegian GI scheme emphasised that the scheme was to apply to products of high quality.[72] In the previous sub-analysis, I showed that administrators consider it challenging to clarify what high quality entails. The same challenge is also raised by consultants and producers. They say that they initiate adaptation work to decide what characteristics will define high quality and how to comply with the definition once the product regulation have been formally approved.

In an interview with a producer and a consultant who represent the same producer organisation, one of the practices that help to ensure high product quality was emphasised. When asked whether production has changed since the requirements for high quality were defined, I was told that it largely remains the same, but that the quality requirements have led to a more stringent sorting of products.

AWH:	Was this how things were done before, or was a bit more cooperation needed to put things in place?
Consultant:	No, when you think about the cultivation technique, things are done in the same way as before.
Producer:	We probably haven't changed the production procedures, but what has changed, or what it has led to, is sorting by quality. So the products sold under that brand have to be tip-top.

In addition to products having to be produced in a specific area, the product regulations also stipulate requirements for other qualities. The transition from being an ordinary traditional product to becoming a product from a specific place also entails setting various criteria for what constitutes high quality. Those that meet the quality criteria are granted GI recognition, while those that do not, are sold without a geographical designation even if they come from the same place. The example thus illustrates how adaptation work in relation to quality criteria contributes to excluding products and producers. For stockfish, for example, only the top two quality categories, *Prima* and *Sekunda*, are deemed to be of sufficient quality to warrant protection.[73] As mentioned, one of the criteria that defines the quality of potatoes is dry matter content. The same applies to *Hardangereple* ('apples from Hardanger'). In order to ensure that the product quality improves, products that do not meet the requirements in the production regulations are sorted out. High-quality products can be further nuanced by dividing them into different varieties. *Rakfisk fra Valdres* and *Fenalår fra Norge* are examples of such products that help to maintain product diversity. While the fermented fish product *Rakfisk* exists in the varieties *Mild, Matured* and *Extramatured*,[74] *Fenalår* (cured leg of mutton) comes in *Traditional* and *Matured* varieties.[75]

Sorting out products that do not meet the quality criteria from the total quantity produced is perhaps the simplest way of adapting products to the product regulations' criteria for high quality. In some cases, however, the situation prior to the application process was that no or only occasional products met the requirements for high quality defined in the product regulations. This shows that the understanding of quality is not exclusively linked to the taste characteristics of the end product. Quality is also associated with the ability to repeatedly produce products of the same quality. Instead of establishing an arrangement whereby the products in a batch that happen to be of high quality are selected from the total produced, the producer organisations make endeavours to control the entire production process and thereby also the quality of the product. In other words, the consultants describe a desired development – from no strict requirements for raw materials, production processes, little final control and a wide range of quality, to stricter requirements for raw materials and production, in addition to a final control in which products that fall within the different quality categories in the product regulations are sorted from each other. The adaptation work has a bearing on the understanding of quality, all the way from the development of regulations to specific provisions about which variant a product can be classified as, or whether it falls outside the set criteria. In other words, more complex adaptation practices are required in cases where high quality is not naturally a frequent occurrence. In this case, such a complex adaptation practice involved working *towards* transformation. In cases where applicants are granted protection under the Norwegian GI scheme, such transformations may have been a key part of the adaptation work.

Transformations and translations of the product and other material factors

> An application for protection of designations of origin and geographical indications shall contain [...] a description of the product with information regarding the raw materials and the most important physical, chemical, microbiological and/or organoleptic characteristics.[76]

The degree of processing the products for which a geographical indication is applied for have undergone varies. For example, there are differences in the degree of processing when comparing dairy products such as *gamalost* and *tjukkmjølk* (thick sour milk) with types of fruit from Hardanger or potatoes from Oppdal, Ringerike and Northern Norway. Regardless of the degree of processing, all producer organisations that apply for a geographical indication must agree on what raw materials can be used and what characteristics the protected product must have. Since the degree of processing differs, such adaptation work presents different challenges. Some organisations have products with similar characteristics that can easily be translated into product regulations. Others have less similar products, in which case transformations will be required in addition to translations. In the quote below, a producer talks about the process of agreeing on the choice of raw materials, taste and production method.

AWH: Did the producers follow an identical recipe?
Producer: No, they didn't, but it was fairly similar, yes it was.
AWH: What were the differences between you?
Producer: Well, it was just minor adjustments of the ingredients that there is not much of. We use something that the others don't, and they use more of something else that we use less of. They use something in their production that we can't get to work in our machines.

AWH: Do they have a machine, too, or do they produce in a different way?

Producer: They have a machine, but not the same type as we do. Their way of doing it is really old school.

AWH: But they have the same packaging as you, right?

Producer: No, it's not the same.

AWH: How was the process of agreeing on a common recipe?

Producer: It was no problem for us to agree, because we realised that the small differences between us, they would be no problem to adjust to, so we agreed.

AWH: Did the others become more like you, or did you become more like them? Or was it something in between?

Producer: Perhaps we adapted more to them, and that was perhaps a little in our best interest. Because we believe that the recipe they had was a bit more like the original one. Because when we started using the machine in our production, we didn't think about being particularly loyal to the old recipe. We had to find something that worked in the new machine and see how the product turned out.

AWH: So you thought that the recipe the other producers had was more original. How could you know that?

Producer: Well, we didn't actually know. But compared to the old recipes that the Norwegian Society of Rural Women have, it looked like their recipe was more like the one we could see the others had than the one we were using at the time. So we adjusted a little more in that direction. It may have changed the flavour a bit, but nothing dramatic, not at all. But we had to agree on a master recipe.

This producer's story is interesting in several ways. Firstly, it illustrates how the material qualities of the means of production have a bearing on the development of food culture. It is important for the producer that the qualities of the ingredients of the product they agree to produce 'worked in the machine' they already have. The material aspect, and implicitly the financial side, thus influences food culture development. In this case, the product was adapted to the machines, but sometimes the opposite is true, for example, when sorting machines have to be adapted to allow the products to be sorted properly. The producer also mentions that they changed the product's recipe while developing the product regulation. This had a bearing on the taste of the product, but the producer emphasised that the differences were only minor and insignificant. The minor changes at product level are thus presented as a result of the reorganisation and the cooperation on common product regulation. Another important thing pointed out by the producer is that they have moved away from the production method that was used until recently. The producer outlines a development where they first changed from traditional production to modern mechanical production. In the second transition, however, they changed back to a more traditional form of mechanical production based on the Norwegian Society of Rural Women's recipes. This and similar cases show how the adaptation work turns the labelling scheme into a tool for reinventing traditions. While this form of adaptation can be understood as *preserving* food culture, transformations that create something new will represent *innovation* (Amilien and Hegnes 2007). From this perspective, the producer's production practice has gone from innovative to preserving. The legitimisation of this conservative approach to the preparation of the product regulation is linked to the Norwegian Society of Rural Women's expertise in the field. Their knowledge is presented as an authentic food tradition, while the material properties of the machines represent the opposite, despite the fact that mechanical production actually contributed to upholding the tradition during a transitional period.

Like the producers, the administrators also perceive the Norwegian GI scheme as highlighting the special while also standardising products that used to be different. Among other things, they point out that the outcome of the adaptation work is twofold. On the one hand, transformations do entail a standardisation of food culture. On the other hand, they promote diversity by preserving something that could have become extinct if the GI scheme had not been established and used. Taken to its logical conclusion, the impression is that traditional products with diminishing popularity are faced with a choice between standardisation or extinction.

The transformation work concerns more than just machines and products, however. It also relates to other material aspects of the Norwegian labelling scheme. For example, some organisations adapt their packaging as well as the product itself. Transformations at product level often have consequences for the design of the material in which the product is packaged, transported and bought. Products that have been granted GI recognition are packaged, labelled and often have a different design than products that do not meet the requirements for a geographical indication. The quality of the products is thereby communicated to the consumer through its packaging. This can be understood in light of what sociologist Franck Cochoy writes about product packaging (2007:120). There are two aspects in particular that can be related to the Norwegian scheme for PDO, PGI, and TSG. The first is that packaging *transforms the qualification of the product.* Cochoy points out that the packaging gives the product an additional materiality that informs and conceals at the same time. The second aspect relates to the first, as this dual materiality enables the *invisible dimensions of products, for instance the presence of a guarantee.* PDO, PGI, and TSG labels are usually placed on the packaging, alternatively on both the product and the packaging. This provides information about the invisible dimensions of the product, for example that it comes from a very specific geographical area. However, there is reason to question whether this information is invisible to all consumers. People who have grown up with particular products will often not need a label to recognise them. Products with geographical indications can thus be understood in light of the opposition between being *embedded and disembedded,* where *locally embedded, alternative food systems are set in opposition to the distantiated, socially disembedded food relations associated with global industrial agriculture* (Bowen 2011:326). In this context, it is only when products go from being *embedded* to becoming *disembedded* that packaging and labelling becomes necessary to reveal the products' invisible characteristics. This varying need for information on packaging is emphasised by the established practice in both Norway and the rest of Europe, where producers that sell their products locally do not use labelling, precisely because the consumers are already familiar with the product. Packaging *with* labelling is used when food is sold outside the local area, in places where people are less familiar with the product (Amilien et al. 2007).

Different kinds of materiality are assigned and have different meanings, both within and between groups of producers, administrators and consumers, and they are adapted in different ways. This is evident, for example, in the question of whether machines should be adapted to the product or the product to the machines. The material conditions appear to entail both opportunities and requirements. The fact that it is actors of flesh and blood who make decisions and feel the consequences of the material adaptation work makes it a socio-material issue (Østerberg 1998). The mutual relationship between the producer organisations' transformations of products and the development and formalisation of product names is another example.

Confirmation and rewriting of product names

An application for protection of designations of origin and geographical indications shall contain [...] the trade name of the product, including the designation of origin or the geographical indication.[77]

Studies have already been conducted on the development of names of Norwegian products that have been granted GI recognition. Examples include Amilien and Hegnes's (2004) review of the development of the name of the fermented fish product known under the protected geographical indication *Rakfisk fra Valdres* and Hegnes's (2007) review of how the cheese *gamalost* developed from a common product from mountain summer pasture farms to a protected geographical indication (*Gamalost frå Vik*).

The product names are often adapted during the course of work on the product regulations. For example, the original name can be combined with a geographical designation. Such changes are not always made, and they need not be problematic. Some organisations simply protect the name that has traditionally been used to refer to their product. Examples include *Skjenning* and *Ringerikserter*. The three different varieties of potatoes that have achieved a geographical indication are, unlike the traditional flatbread Skjenning and peas from Ringerike, examples of adaptation work and the rewriting, or adaptation, of product names.[78]

The potato variety now granted protection under the name *Ringerikspotet fra Ringerike* ('Ringerikspotet from Ringerike') was previously mostly referred to simply as *Ringerikspotet*. Correspondingly, the potato variety protected under the name *Gulløye fra Nord-Norge* ('Gulløye from Northern Norway') was previously simply called *Gulløye* or *Gullauge*. *Mandelpotet fra Oppdal* ('almond potatoes from Oppdal') underwent a process that ended with the protected geographical indication *Fjellmandel fra Oppdal* ('mountain almond potatoes from Oppdal'). For the *Ringerikspotet* variety, another geographical designation was added to the one that was already part of the established name. *Gulløye* also had a geographical area included in its name, but this area was not previously consistently associated with *Gulløye*. For *Mandelpotet*, the geographical name 'Oppdal' was supplemented with the generic designation 'fjell' ('mountain'). While Oppdal refers to the geographical area, the reference to mountain specifies another criterium, namely elevation above sea level. Section 3(2) of the product regulation specify what is meant by 'mountain':

> Geographical area: Fjellmandel fra Oppdal must be grown in Oppdal municipality limited to areas more than 400 metres above sea level.[79]

As mentioned above, the requirement that potatoes with geographical indications be of high quality has also resulted in specific requirements concerning dry matter content. The transition from being an ordinary *mandelpotet* (almond potato) to becoming a *mandelpotet* from a specific location takes place through a sorting process based on tests of material properties such as size, dry matter content, colour etc. Those who meet the material quality criteria are granted immaterial property rights in the form of a geographical indication, while potatoes that do not meet the requirements are sold with no geographical designation even if they come from the same field. The material, immaterial, and social aspects of this process are closely interrelated. The dry matter content and protected name represent the material and immaterial aspects, respectively. Ownership of the product name is also linked to social groups with financial interests. This naming of products with certain material properties and geographical origins is also closely linked to how the name is communicated through logos and packaging labelled with symbols.

Power shifts in connection with the adaptation of labelling

An application for protection of designations of origin and geographical indications shall contain [...] proposals for labelling the product.[80]

The assumption underlying the preparatory works was that both the regulations themselves and the logos would be modelled on the EU system.[81] The logos that symbolise the different categories of protection in Norway and in the EU are shown below.[82] The reason why there are two EU logos in the PDO category is that the symbol shown on the third line replaced the one on the second line in 2008. The reason for this development was that the first three

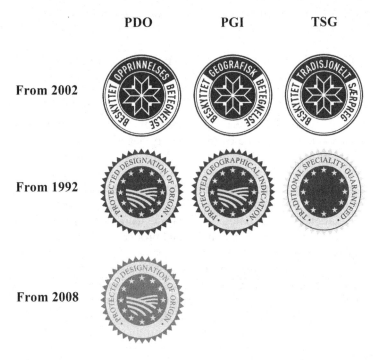

Figure 2.2 Label logos from Norway and the EU.

were deemed to be too similar to properly communicate the distinction between the different forms of protection. The EU logos bear the stars from the EU flag. The Norwegian logos have a single star, or rose, from the knitted design known as the *Selbu* pattern. In both cases, the form of protection is specified in writing.

The Norwegian logos are inspired by different models. On the one hand, the EU scheme has had model power. However, the Norwegian scheme and logos was also developed modelled on symbols in Norwegian culture, other national expertise and in consultation with affected Norwegian stakeholders. The development of the Norwegian label can be said to be characterised by an adaptation process that was somewhere between translation and transformation – translation because the Norwegian symbol is intended to communicate the same meaning in the context of the Norwegian market and food culture as the EU symbols do in the EU, and transformation because the actual design of the symbols is different.

Since the symbols and the regulations were adopted in Norway, special guidelines have been drawn up for the use of logos and product designations.[83] These guidelines must be followed when producer organisations prepare proposals for product labelling in connection with their applications. Some quickly agree on how their products should be labelled, while other organisations need more time. The adaptation work sometimes prove challenging, for example because some producers want to keep their original names. Challenges sometimes arise when administrators nonetheless encourage producers to agree on common labelling for their organisation in their applications.

Producer: Well, yes, in our opinion, the tradition is actually that there are many names. Preserving these names is just as important a part of the cultural tradition as making up a new name because the regulations say that we have to. If you want to preserve culture, you really can't force it to fit a set of regulations. But it is difficult to get the people who make the decisions to understand that it's actually a question of food, concepts and culture.

Producers in this producer organisation did not want to relinquish their own names for a new, common name and common labelling. They were worried about losing the reputation that each of them had already built up over a long period of time. The Norwegian scheme for PDO, PGI and TSG can thereby be counterproductive when all names are 'forced to fit a set of regulations' and come out the other end with a single geographical indication. The reorganisation of producers is thus linked to the development of product designations and labelling. The producers would rather retain their diversity than adapt to the public administration's requirement to agree on name and labelling. In such cases, the administrators exercise what I have previously referred to as guidance power in their attempts to guide the producers towards agreement on a common label. In this case, the producer resisted, which illustrates the shifting and complex nature of the power relations that play out between guidance power and producer autonomy.

Other producers are concerned with the significance of the labelling and how important it will be whether or not they use the symbol. In such cases, some organisations demonstrate autonomy by deciding how to label their products within the limits set by the scheme.

However, it is not always the case that producers who have achieved GI recognition decide the packaging design and product labelling alone. Some producers state that they decide the packaging and logos as long as they sell products from their own farm. The situation changes when they sell them via a wholesaler, as wholesalers demand that their logo be used instead of the logo of the producer organisation. This situation can be described using Weber's concept of *Macht*, as wholesalers seem to get their way when it comes to packaging and logos. The power relations in the value chain become evident in such cases. In this perspective, who decides the packaging and labelling can be understood to constitute part of what is referred to as *food power* (Rommetvedt 2002; Bilden 2011; NOU 2011:4). Specifically, it can be understood as a sub-category of food power called *brand power*.

A nuanced example of the relationship between adaptation and brand power was given in an interview during which I was shown packaging from before and after a product was granted GI recognition. I noticed that the organisation had chosen the black and white version of the symbol label and asked about the reason for this choice.

Consultant: Here is the version with the protected label.
AWH: Is there a reason why you don't use the symbol in blue?

Consultant:	Yes, there is. A design firm created it for us. I think we decided that the blue colour conflicted a bit with the motifs, which they spent a great deal of time on.
AWH:	Yes, they are very nice.
Consultant:	Yes, so it was sort of by recommendation. We thought about how it would look, and then we arrived at that, but whether that is final, we don't know – time will tell.

It thus emerged that the organisation or consultant had taken advice about the choice of packaging and the colour of the symbol. Graphic designers have guidance power in such situations. The consultant states that the producer organisation has the final word, however. This emphasis on the autonomy of the producer organisation in labelling matters tallies with the description from the organisation that sold its products via a wholesaler. The shifting nature of power relations is apparent when producers and consultants emphasise that other parties as well as themselves have a say in decisions concerning labelling and packaging.

The preceding examples relate to adaptation work and power in the relationship between the autonomy of producer organisations and other actors such as the EU, administrators, wholesalers, and designers. In addition, internal power relations within the producer organisations can also have a bearing on the adaptation of symbols and packaging.

Product labelling and packaging trigger a number of different adaptation practices and serve as a good example of how the food-cultural adaptation work linked to the use of the Norwegian GI scheme is characterised by shifting power relations. Adaptations of labelling and packaging are accompanied by different forms of brand power in the relationships between the EU and Norway, producers and the public administration, producers and wholesalers, producers and designers, and internally between producers. The power relations can be interpreted on the basis of the three forms of power I have already introduced. While wholesalers exercise *Macht*, guidance power is associated with administrators and designers. The EU has model power and sets guidelines for the development of symbols. There are other power relations in addition to the three I have just mentioned. For example, there is no doubt that consultants possess and exercise power in the adaptation work.

When producers go from producing separately to agreeing on a product regulation, while cooperating as a new organisation, they have to reach agreement on new names and on how their products are to be labelled. The organisations also have to decide on the delimitation of the geographical area for the cultivation, production, and processing of the products that will be covered by the label.

Localisations and re-localisations of geographical areas

> An application for protection of designations of origin and geographical indications shall contain [...] a definition of the geographical area.[84]

The delimitation of the geographical area is an important part of adaptation work. The area agreed upon must be relatable to the products and suit the needs of the producers, comply with the framework regulation and satisfy those who interpret and enforce them. Some find it easy to agree on where the raw materials and products can come from, but in the excerpt below, a consultant describes an instance when that was not the case. The producers, and perhaps most of all the consultant himself, found the adaptation and delimitation of the geographical area so difficult that it nearly resulted in them giving up on the whole collaboration on the application.

AWH: What did you consider most challenging?

Consultant: Well, I don't really know what was most challenging. It's a pretty demanding process, to be honest. One thing is to describe a product regulation that you know that the enterprises can and will follow up later. At the same time, if you're going to guarantee something, it shouldn't be an easy solution, such approval should be difficult to achieve. Perhaps in a way, with so many producers and different traditions for how to source the raw materials and process them and then somehow end up with a product regulation that everyone can get behind.

AWH: So there were many conversations with the producers before this?

Consultant: Yes, there were many conversations with the enterprises!

AWH: Was there a very big difference in how they did things before?

Consultant: You can say that the biggest challenge – which nearly torpedoed the entire process, simply got us to abandon the work. That was the issue of where the raw materials could come from.

The consultant reasons that the greatest challenge was where the raw materials for the product could come from, i.e. the delimitation of the geographical area. This delimitation process can, as shown in the quote above, be difficult in situations where there is internal disagreement between producers that have to adapt to each other. In a worst-case scenario, this could cause the adaptation process to break down completely.

In other cases, adaptation challenges concern the point of departure for the delimitation. One way of delimiting the geographical area is to take human knowledge and natural conditions as one's point of departure. This form of adaptation practice takes the food culture as the point of departure and draws maps and boundaries that coincide with it. This is the form of delimitation that I refer to as *localisation*. *Ringerikserter* ('peas from Ringerike') is an example of a delimitation that is largely based on the landscape, which is also clear from the product regulation.

> **Geographical area:** The area for production, processing and preparation of Ringerikserter is defined as the Røyse peninsula in Hole municipality, limited by the Tyrifjord in the east, south and vest and the climate conservation zone and the present military area in the north and north-east.[85]

Another, opposite adaptation practice takes existing maps and boundaries as its point of departure. In other words, this way of adapting the geographical delimitation entails adapting the food culture to the maps and *re-locating* the food culture accordingly. Challenges sometimes arise as a result of differences of opinion about the point of departure for geographical delimitation – i.e.

whether to *locate* or *re-locate*. One informant describes such a situation in which the administrators encouraged them to use the municipal borders rather than the food-cultural boundaries, which, according to the producer, follow valleys:

AWH: You said something I would be interested in hearing more about. The delimitation of the area. Was it a difficult process to achieve that?

Producer: Yes, it was a little difficult to document where the boundaries were, but we finally managed that too. But what was a bit of a problem, was that they (administrators) weren't happy that we split a municipality in two when setting the boundaries.

AWH: No?

Producer: But we believed that was how it should be. In a municipality with two different valleys, one of them can have a tradition for making the product while the other one doesn't. So we felt that the boundary had to be drawn between them, but it wasn't approved that we split the municipality. The boundaries are slightly at odds with what we believe has been the area where the product was used. But, at the same time, the boundaries have expanded a bit, so it is a question of when you should say that the boundaries applied.

AWH: So they would prefer you to follow the municipal borders?

Producer: Yes, when we talked about the product's geographical origin, we had to use the name of the municipality. So the boundaries ended up a little different from what we envisaged.

This example describes a re-location of the tradition in the work on the product regulation. An area defined by food-cultural practice is re-located to the present municipal borders, which are easy for the public administration to relate to and enforce.

The norm in the EU and Norway is to limit geographical indications to a local area or region. The EU regulation explicitly refers to delimitation at country level as the exception. Article 2 of the EU regulation states that:

'designation of origin'/'geographical indication' means the name of a region, a specific place or, in exceptional cases, a country, used to describe an agricultural product or a foodstuff.[86]

The Norwegian scheme for PDO, PGI and TSG is adapted to accommodate Norwegian food culture's strong national focus, however. There is already one product approved with Norway as the approved area[87] and one that is based on the entire coast of Norway, but with further delimitation. The geographical delimitations for *Fenalår fra Norge* ('cured leg of mutton from Norway') and *Villsau frå Norskekysten* ('wild sheep from the Norwegian coast') are described as follows in their respective product regulations:

Fenalår fra Norge must be produced, processed and prepared in Norway.[88]

The geographical area for the production of Villsau frå Norskekysten is limited to coastal heathland along the coast of Norway.[89]

While delimitation through location and re-location is characterised by local/regional exclusion and inclusion, the adaptation work when the geographical delimitation is Norway as a whole is more unambiguously characterised by national inclusion. To summarise, we can say that the delimitation of geographical areas is practised through locations and re-locations that can be understood as variants of translation, and that they are characterised by degrees of exclusion and inclusion. For PDO and PGI, requirements are stipulated concerning the extent to which products can be said to be produced, processed, and prepared within a defined area. This means that there is also a link between place and production method.[90]

Synchronisation and reorganisation of production methods

An application for protection of designations of origin and geographical indications shall contain [...] a description of the method used to produce the product.[91]

Producers that apply for a geographical indication must agree on the production method. In some cases, this is unproblematic because the producers behind the application already do things in the same way. Other cases are more complicated.

Producer organisations can translate their own history and production practices themselves, or they can outsource this work to others. Sometimes, there are fairly close connections between the producers and the consultants engaged to write the application. In other cases, the relationship is more distant. The knowledge and expertise of consultants are factors that contribute to the success of this process. Perhaps they have been involved in the type of production for which they write applications. They may also have other experience of working in local experimental societies where their duties involved contact with the authorities, organisation work and project management. Such dual production and management experience could be the reason why a consultant is given responsibility for the translation, but it will also be a big help in the actual work of translating production methods into regulations.

Sometimes, agreeing on a production method is more of a challenge. In producer organisations with both big and small producers among their members, for example, there could be different ways of practising production, which requires painstaking adaptation work. For example, the differences could relate to the material production conditions. A consultant describes the experience of endeavouring to reach agreement on the production method in such a producer organisation:

Consultant:	Each producer has their own way of doing things and believes that is the best way. That is the point of departure. And there are both big and small producers, which also gives rise to problems.
AWH:	What is the difference between big and small producers? What is it the small ones want that the big ones don't?
Consultant:	The main difference is that the big ones often have optimal equipment to produce in the best possible way. The small ones are much more at the mercy of nature because they don't have climate-controlled chambers with optimal conditions.
AWH:	Yes, I see. How many of the big ones have climate-controlled chambers?

Consultant: The big ones all have them. And there are differences between them too, by all means, but many of the small ones just have to rely on nature. And that's the traditional way, really.

Reaching agreement on the production method is difficult for an organisation that includes both big and small producers. The producer organisation has an underlying wish to unite tradition with quality. However, consultants indicate that this may be difficult because the requirements for tradition and quality could come into conflict with each other. The consultant states that modern equipment is required to meet the requirements for high quality, while the tradition is based on 'relying on nature'. In some cases, highly controlled systems such as climate-controlled chambers are used to achieve good quality, but when the tradition is not to use such chambers, things become complicated. Later in the same interview, this is expressed more explicitly:

Consultant: Striking that balance, that was something we struggled with for months. Finding out how to deal with the diversity, rooting it in history and tradition and sort of balancing that bit while making a quality product at the same time. We had several rounds of discussions.

In the interviews, adaptation work is frequently described as involving several rounds of discussions. This consultant has first had several rounds of discussions with big and small producers to reach agreement. Afterwards, there may be additional rounds with the Norwegian Food Branding Foundation and the Norwegian Food Safety Authority. This whole discussion is directly relevant to the adaptation work, including translations and transformations. Consultants are tasked with translating a complex tradition into a set of regulations in cooperation with producers and administrators. Material conditions are also relevant to this practice. Big and small producers must consider material transformations if they are to be able to make products that meet the requirements that they themselves have taken part in drawing up. Small producers must consider using climate-controlled chambers to achieve high quality, and big producers must consider more manual work to satisfy traditional sorting and production methods. There is an interplay between the two forms of adaptation work.

Generally speaking, it is a challenge to adapt and translate knowledge passed down through generations into legal language. One of the producers elaborates on this in response to a question about the transition from non-recorded to recorded knowledge. In the excerpt below, I am particularly eager to find out whether the product regulation reflect what the actual production practices have been like, or whether something has been lost during the dialogue with the Norwegian Food Branding Foundation.

AWH: You've been producing in this way for many years now. Then you submit an application to the Norwegian Food Branding Foundation: 'This is how we've done it'. And then maybe the Norwegian Food Branding Foundation says: 'That won't work'. How does that feel?

Producer: We think it's sheer madness, really … It's just one of those … It's a definition thing, to put it that way. And we feel that we are the practitioners here, right, we sit here and know that it has always been grown and always been done that way. And then someone with a more legal background comes along and tries to fit it into a different system. It's sort of about making those two things go together, in a way. But we think that that's how things are, I suppose, and we'll just have to try to word it in a way that fits the system, so that it works in relation to the regulations.

AWH: But is anything lost in the process? I mean, when you take all the knowledge you have and write it down in your way, in dialogue with legal advisers in the Norwegian Food Branding Foundation or the Norwegian Food Safety Authority, does anything sort of get lost, or is what the regulations say, what has been the essence of the tradition so far?

Producer: I think it's fine, I think it is the essence that's there as the foundation, and we know the rest, to put it that way. We know, it's there, and then it is a regulation.

AWH: But there must be a lot of practical aspects that aren't included in the regulations? I am thinking about manual skills and such?

Producer: Yes, there are lots of things. But it's good that we have written it down, how to do things, in the regulations.

The producer is happy to have succeeded in drafting a product regulation but makes no secret of the fact that such a product regulation cannot convey all the practical aspects of production. Notwithstanding the objective of translating tacit knowledge into product regulations, part of the knowledge will remain tacit. In light of this, it may be interesting to think in terms of one form of knowledge being more or less tacit than another. When ranking knowledge by how tacit it can be, the most tacit form of knowledge will be the practical know-how that is not described in the product regulations.

The producers describe a process characterised by dialogue with administrators whereby they have reached a kind of agreement. The producer is nevertheless ambivalent when it comes to communicating knowledge in new language. On the one hand, it is described as challenging work. On the other, the system is accepted, and the adaptation work is perceived as positive. Different actors display different degrees of this ambiguous attitude.

The skills required to reorganise, translate and transform are important to how the application process develops. While some have reorganisation skills, others may be skilled in documentation work, and yet others can easily make material changes to the products or production that help to keep the process moving forward. Some producer organisations possess translation skills in the form of staff who are familiar both with the production and the legislation. These consultants are an important resource in the application work.

Despite assistance from consultants, the producers describe a sometimes difficult application process involving disagreement between the producer organisation and the public administration. Among other things, the producers and consultants mention the Norwegian Food Branding Foundation being unable to put itself in the producers' position, the relationship between European and translated Norwegian regulations, that the regulations are rigid, that the producers themselves have to teach the Norwegian Food Branding Foundation how the system works, the ability to see past the regulations, and that producers also have a network and consultants that help them with case processing, for example by looking to Southern Europe for examples they can use to support their arguments. This touches on several facets of the translation work. Although the producers and the public administration disagree, they have to adapt and put themselves in the other party's position in order to translate the production method into regulations. A producer gave a general description of what happens in the *interaction between the law and us who work 'on the shop floor, so to speak'* in an application process. Although these reflections are more general in nature, they nevertheless describe what happens when the production method is described in applications for product regulations. The producer points out that it is difficult to put oneself in the other party's position, but that it is crucial in order to succeed in achieving GI recognition.

The review of the adaptation work done to describe the production method shows considerable diversity. It is not sufficient to achieve GI recognition simply to document how things are done, however. You also have to document where they are done and where the product originates from.

Reorganisations, transformations, and traceability

An application for protection of designations of origin and geographical indications shall contain [...] information that confirms that the product originates in the specified geographical area.[92]

The experience of adapting to the conditions concerning traceability varies, both within and between producer organisations. Some find it easy because they already have procedures in place that ensure good traceability. Other organisations find it more challenging because the different producers have different systems, resources and strategies in this area. Among other things, it is clear that big and small producers differ in terms of traceability systems and capabilities. Big producers run the risk of having to reorganise their work and transform equipment to comply with traceability requirements. The small producers appear to find this condition less challenging, and they have no great need for adaptation work other than to translate their traceability procedures into a description in the application.

It is not uncommon for producers to say that they did not fully realise what is required in connection with an application for GI recognition. Another aspect of adaptation work is linked to the consultants' work on translating the meaning of the regulations and the criteria for the producers, among other things. In such cases, the challenge facing the consultant is to translate the conditions for the producers in such a way that they understand that it is possible to adapt to such a requirement during the course of the application process.

The traceability requirements, like other conditions, have changed over time, a fact that one producer mentions in connection with an application that has been under consideration for a long time:

Producer: There was some re-writing because there had been some changes relating to KSL and tracing. We had to change it a little. There was a little of that and some little things that they started with …

AWH: After the merger between Matmerk and KSL?

Producer: I don't know if it was after the merger or if the traceability requirements had changed, but it was 'peanuts'.

The excerpt above suggests that the merger between the Norwegian Food Branding Foundation and the Norwegian Quality System for Agriculture[93] led to new conditions for a product regulation that had nearly been completed. Adaptation work is triggered by reorganisations in the public administration that bring new traceability requirements, which in turn require the product regulation to be re-written.

Despite some challenges, the traceability conditions appear to be relatively easy for producer organisations to adapt to compared with the condition that requires the effects of natural and human factors on the quality of the product to be documented.

Writing, re-writing, and translation of the food-people-places nexus

An application for protection of designations of origin and geographical indications shall contain […] specification of the factors that bear out the link with the geographical environment or the geographical origin.[94]

It emerged in the analysis of the administration of the Norwegian GI scheme that the administrators find the condition requiring producers to specify factors that demonstrate the product's link to the geographical area particularly challenging. In more concrete terms, 'factors' means links between the natural and human factors' impact on the finished product. Most are aware of these links, but many find it difficult to put this knowledge, which is often deeply tacit, into words. The application work requires taking epistemological steps to transition from tacit/non-reflexive to reflexive knowledge, and then on to formulation and translation into regulations. Once the regulations are in place, maintenance work is required, as a consultant points out:

Consultant: Later, and after we were granted recognition, we have gone into more detail about it and explained and talked about it at meetings with the producers, because it needs to become second nature for them too.

Writing down the history of the products is also an important contribution to documenting links in the application work. Several of the products did not have a written history before. This work therefore has to be done during the application process. It is not just the histories that are written from scratch, but they are also written by new history writers in cooperation with the Norwegian Food Branding Foundation. The conditions stipulated in the regulations make their mark on the product histories, and the Norwegian Food Branding Foundation has influence over what is and is not an acceptable and workable history. The new histories that are written down are thereby a product of the adaptation work.

There are also examples of producers who told me that they did not understand the language used by the administrators or the conditions that the administrators tried to communicate as regards geographical links. To the producers, their tradition is so self-evident that they find it difficult to communicate what it is that makes it special. They also find it difficult to understand what the administrators are asking for. The combination of not being able to successfully communicate and not understanding the conditions makes for very challenging adaptation work. A clearer understanding of the conditions can sometimes be achieved by talking directly with representatives of the Norwegian Food Branding Foundation, however.

The producers are by no means completely new to paperwork, but drafting product regulations is still a new experience for them. The producers have to think in new ways and put tacit knowledge into words. We can draw a parallel between this and the administrators' work on adapting the Norwegian framework regulation as far as possible to the EU scheme. This approach entails a risk of administrators becoming too distant and alienated from the Norwegian regulations. However, when all the national conditions are incorporated into the text as reservations and exceptions, it is clear that the map matches the Norwegian food culture terrain better, and a form of balance arises. Producers are also concerned with how to ensure that this balance is struck, and some express dissatisfaction with the model power of France and Italy, which they believe have too strong a position in the adaptation work:

Producer: No, but ... I don't know, it's precisely that underlying value dimension that is particular to craft production. We build our production on a rich history, right? We have an authentic foundation for the production, it has been handed down to us from generation to generation, so this is the craft production that is rooted in this area. And that was how it was produced. And you don't just buy a product, but you buy a product with a rich history going back to the women who used to prepare food for weddings and similar events in their local community. So it has to do with roots and origin, and what is supposed to be the authentic origin of this food culture. And what was it like, and what was it based on? And then it's important for us to stick to the principles and values that the local women who made it have passed down to us. And that, those differences, you know, we find that to be a hard sell when dealing with the Norwegian Food Branding Foundation, and they sort of use the labelling scheme as a framework, and they see it as a strategy, and they say that that's what is written in the laws and regulations, and that's how it's practised in France and Italy. We, little Norway, right? We are four million people in this country. And, you know, there are some differences here that I find it difficult to make directly transferable to Norwegian society, although the goal of this

> geographical indication scheme is very good, the whole idea of drawing attention to treasured foods, old treasured foods. But it is a bit problematic to get them to be a little flexible in relation to the legal side, I find.

The above quote points to two different levels of translation work. On the one level, it involves translating established knowledge and tradition into product regulation, while, on the other, it concerns aspects of the process of translating the European system for Norwegian conditions. The translation work related to the Norwegian scheme for PDO, PGI, and TSG is not limited to these levels, however. When considering the scheme as a whole, it is clear that translations between different fields/discourses/levels are, and have been, crucial to the development of the labelling scheme.

Some find it easy to translate their understanding of the link between the natural and human factors' impact on the product they produce. For others, this adaptation work requires them to think about their own production and product in a way that they are not familiar with. This adaptation work primarily relates to the aspect of meaning. One of the most important functions of the scheme is precisely to imbue products with a certain meaning by adapting them and ensuring that they come from a specific place, a specific natural environment and that they are produced by certain people in a certain way.

In sum

Producers undertake extensive food-cultural adaptation work when they choose to work towards GI recognition. In this sub-analysis, I have shown how adaptation work is necessary to meet the most important conditions in the framework regulation in applications for GI recognition and when developing product regulations. As in the two preceding sub-analyses, I have shown the significance of the different adaptation practices separately, as well as how they interact with each other and can be understood as chains of adaptations. In addition to the three most important adaptation practices, I have also felt a need to point out some additional ones in order to nuance and comprehend the complexity of the adaptation work. The producers' use of the Norwegian GI scheme is characterised by more diverse adaptation work compared with the period of introduction and the administration of the scheme. The reason for this is that the producers have to utilise all the three most important adaptation practices, as well as a number of other ones. They have to translate their deeply tacit and traditional knowledge, reorganise into new groups, and transform their products.

I have described and analysed the use of the Norwegian GI scheme in terms of cultural adaptation work and the elements such an approach comprises. Using this analytical approach, I found that the most prominent cultural differences in the use of the Norwegian GI scheme are related to meaning, organisation, and material conditions. According to the framework regulation, product names without a geographical designation have a different meaning than names with such a designation. This has triggered re-writes. Producer organisations have not always been organised in the way assumed by the Norwegian GI scheme, which triggers reorganisations. When products initially fail to meet the material requirements for high quality, that triggers transformations. As in the administration of the scheme, the most prominent actors in its use are producers, consultants, and administrators. Other actors are also involved, however. The actors represent a broader range of knowledge and adaptive competence in the use of the Norwegian GI scheme than they did during its preparations and in its administration. The producers have to familiarise themselves with the legal framework and take their tacit knowledge about their production practices and products to a new reflexive level when drawing up the product regulations. Use of the Norwegian GI scheme gives rise to an interplay between translations, reorganisations and transformations to compensate for the various cultural differences. Adaptation practices also take a number of other forms. Like during the scheme's introduction and in connection with its administration, adaptation work related to the use of the scheme fundamentally takes place along the order/disorder dimension, as well as the global/local and tradition/innovation dimensions. The power aspect is also a recurring theme in the producers' application work. Shifting power relations in the process of designing the packaging and labelling is one example. Different forms of power are at play in the use of the GI scheme, as well as in its administration. The power dynamics between the producers and other actors help the use of the Norwegian GI scheme to progress. Use of the scheme mostly relates to the same contextual conditions as its adminis-tration. This means that use of the Norwegian scheme is part of the quality turn and must be understood in light of this process and other contextual conditions, including different institutions where science, law and financial considerations can be said to play a particularly prominent role. As I have already mentioned – the collective and individual adaptive force created around the Norwegian GI scheme is linked to an understanding of and wish to bring order to what initially appeared to be disordered.

The adaptation work carried out in connection with the use of the Norwegian GI scheme has several different consequences. Those who do the work have both positive and negative experiences, and it contributes to varying degrees of inclusion and exclusion. The most important adaptation practices used in adaptation work contribute to products and packaging being transformed and to the actors' understanding and organisations changing. Different adaptation practices use different points of departure when deciding a product's geographical origin. This has a bearing on who can achieve GI recognition, among other things. The adaptation work contributes in various ways to raising quality and developing new varieties. At the same time, cooperation between producers entails a degree of standardisa-tion. Food traditions both develop and become more fixed. The consequences of adaptation work thus fluctuate between simi-larity and diversity, preservation and innovation, and between standardisation and extinction. Shifting power relations are a nat-ural consequence of, and perhaps also a prerequisite for, the adap-tation work. This means that several actors have an impact on the outcome of the different forms of adaptation work. Another consequence of the adaptation work is that it 'forces' producers to put their tacit knowledge into words. Sometimes, this means that the history of a product is written down for the first time or re-written. A divide emerges between those who possess adaptive competence and those who do not. There is also a divide between producer organisations that can afford to engage the services of persons with adaptive competence and those that do not have the funds required.

In the final chapter, I present and elaborate on my overall conclu-sion and delve more systematically into the various consequences and implications of adaptation work.[95]

Research literature and other sources

Notes

1 This was one of the expressed goals when the Ministry of Agriculture staff went on a study trip to Paris to learn about origin labelling in France (Ministry of Agriculture (2000) 'Opprinnelsesmerking (AOC) i Frankrike – Rapport fra studietur 27.–30. juni 2000 (in appendix 1)' ('Origin labelling (AOC) in France – Report from study trip 27–30 June 2000' – in Norwegian only), *regjeringen.no,* www.regjeringen.no/ nb/dep/lmd/dok/rapporter-and-planer/rapporter/2000/opprinnelses merking-aoc-i-frankrike-.html?id=277351 (read on 20 October 2010)).

2 Brekk, L. P. (2009) 'Tale for Norsk sau and geit – Fagorganisasjonen for sau- and geiteholdere' ('Speech to the Norwegian Association of Sheep and Goat Farmers' – in Norwegian only), *regjeringen.no,* www. regjeringen.no/nb/dep/lmd/aktuelt/taler_artikler/ministeren/landbr uks--and-matminister-lars-peder-bre/2009/innlegg-mote-hos-norsk-sau-and-geit-.html?id=573325 (read on 19 October 2010).

3 Proposition No 128 to the Storting (1988–1989), p. 39.

4 Proposition No 112 to the Storting (1989–1990), p. 51.

5 Recommendation No 253 to the Storting (1989–1990), pp. 9–10.

6 The committee that prepared this report was appointed already in November 1987.

7 NOU 1991:2B, p. 125.

8 Proposition No 1 to the Storting. Appendix No 1 (1990–1991), p. 81.

9 Proposition No 8 to the Storting (1992–1993).

10 Proposition No 8 to the Storting (1992–1993), p. 28.

11 The Ministry of Agriculture 1992:21.

12 The Ministry of Agriculture 1992:19.

13 The Ministry of Agriculture 1992:22.

14 The scheme was phased out in 2006/2007. For details about the phasing-out, see *Matmerk – norske matmerker, Aktivitetsrapport 2006. ('Norwegian Food Branding Foundation, activity report 2006'– in Norwegian only)*

15 The Ministry of Agriculture 1992:22.

16 NOU 1996:10, p. 88.

17 Report No 40 to the Storting (1996–1997), p. 28.

18 Report No 19 to the Storting (1999–2000), pp. 78–79.

19 Report No 19 to the Storting (1999–2000), p. 104.

20 See, e.g.: Ministry of Fisheries, Ministry of Health, Ministry of Agriculture, in collaboration with the Ministry of Children and Family Affairs (2004) 'Handlingsplan for forbrukerretting av matpolitikken 2004–2005' ('Action plan for consumer orientation of food policy

2004–2005' – in Norwegian only), *regjeringen.no*, www.regjeringen.no/
upload/kilde/ld/rap/2004/0003/ddd/pdfv/209925-handlingsplan_mat_
110504.pdf (read on 20.10.2010).

21 However, Rem also writes that '*Consumers suffer simultaneously from a lack of information and an information overload*' (2008:62), a criticism it is also easy to apply to the Norwegian scheme for PDO, PGI and TSG. As mentioned, the labelling scheme can get lost in the jungle of labels, with few people having the knowledge or interest required to familiarise themselves with its implications.

22 Recommendation No 167 to the Storting (1999–2000), p. 10.

23 Proposition No 82 to the Storting (1999–2000), p. 57.

24 Proposition No 82 to the Storting (1999–2000), p. 66.

25 From the preface to the Ministry of Agriculture (2000) 'Opprinnelsesmerking (AOC) i Frankrike – Rapport fra studietur 27.–30. juni 2000' ('Origin labelling (AOC) in France – Report from study trip 27–30 June 2000' – in Norwegian only), *regjeringen.no*, www.regj eringen.no/nb/dep/lmd/dok/rapporter-and-planer/rapporter/2000/ opprinnelsesmerking-aoc-i-frankrike-.html?id=277351 (read on 20 Oct. 2010).

26 Several studies have pointed to adaptation challenges associated with the introduction of the scheme for PDO, PGI and TSG and *terroir* in countries and food cultures: Poland (Bowen and De Master 2011) and Turkey (Albayrak and Gunes 2010) are examples of the former, while the USA (Paxon 2010) is given as an example of the introduction of *terroir*.

27 *Aftenposten* (2009) 'Eksklusivt matmerke helt ukjent' ('Exclusive food label completely unknown') News p. 7, 24 June 2009.

28 Commission of the European Communities (2008) 'Green paper on agricultural product quality: product standards, farming requirements and quality schemes' (p. 15), *europa.eu*, http://eur-lex.europa.eu/Lex UriServ/LexUriServ.do?uri=COM:2008:0641:FIN:EN:PDF (read on 7 Jan. 2012).

29 European Commission – Directorate-General for Agriculture and Rural Development (2009) 'Conclusions from the consultation on agricultural product quality' (s. 15), *europa.eu*, http://ec.europa.eu/agri culture/quality/policy/consultation/contributions/summary_en.pdf (read on 7 Jan. 2012).

30 Ministry of Agriculture (2000) Consultation letter ref. 99/02486, Date: 21 December 2000.

31 Value Creation Programme for Food Production (2001:6).

32 See pages 5, 6, 9, 12, 13 and 16.

33 Ministry of Agriculture and Food (2005) 'Mat: Lettere å starte småskalaproduksjon' ('Food: Easier to start small-scale production' – in

Norwegian only), *regjeringen.no*, www.regjeringen.no/nb/dokumentar
kiv/Regjeringen-Bondevik-II/Landbruks--and-matdepartementet/233
194/2005/mat-lettere_a_starte_smaskalaproduksjon.html?id=258179
(read on 12 Sept. 2011).
34 Ministry of Agriculture and Food (2010) 'VSP mat etter 2010?
Virkemidler til verdiskaping, innovasjon and mangfold på matområdet'
('Value Creation Programme for Food Production after 2010? Policy
instruments for value creation, innovation and diversity in the food
sector' – in Norwegian only) (p. 9), *regjeringen.no*, www.regjeringen.
no/upload/LMD/Vedlegg/Brosjyrer_veiledere_rapporter/Rapport_
VSP_mat_etter_2010.pdf (read on 6 Jan. 2013).
35 The Norwegian Labour Party, the Socialist Left Party and the
Centre Party (2005) 'Plattform for regjeringssamarbeidet mellom
Arbeiderpartiet, Sosialistisk Venstreparti and Senterpartiet, 2005-09'
('Platform for the government coalition between the Labour Party, the
Socialist Left Party and the Centre Party, 2005–2009' – in Norwegian
only), *regjeringen.no*, www.regjeringen.no/upload/SMK/Vedlegg/2005/
regjeringsplatform_SoriaMoria.pdf (read on 6 Jan. 2013).
36 The Norwegian Labour Party, the Socialist Left Party and the Centre
Party (2009) 'Politisk plattform for flertallsregjeringen utgått av
Arbeiderpartiet, Sosialistisk Venstreparti and Senterpartiet, 2009–
2013', ('Political platform for the majority government formed by the
Labour Party, the Socialist Left Party and the Centre Party, 2009–
2013' – in Norwegian only) *regjeringen.no*, www.regjeringen.no/upl
oad/SMK/Vedlegg/2009/Ny_politisk_plattform_2009-2013.pdf (read
on 6 Jan. 2013).
37 This delimitation and definition work has been ongoing since before
the scheme was introduced until the present. This was confirmed in
an interview with Nina Sundquist in autumn 2012. *Locally sourced.
Locally produced. Small-scale. Traditional food. Organic. Farm product.
These are only some of the terms and designations that are bandied
about when people talk about the new food wave that is washing over
Norway. What do they all mean, and how are they related? 'That isn't
quite clear yet, we are in the process of defining many of the terms,'
says Sundqvist. She is the head of Matmerk – the Norwegian Food
Branding Foundation, whose remit includes labelling of Norwegian food*
(*Aftenposten* (2012) 'Merket mat til å stole på' ('Labelled food can be
trusted' – in Norwegian only). Innsikt supplement p. 12, 11 Oct. 2012).
38 Document 8:96 (2000–2001).
39 Recommendation No 270 to the Storting (2000–2001), enclosure: letter
from the Minister of Agriculture dated 10 May 2001.
40 Ministry of Agriculture and Food (2010) 'VSP mat etter 2010?
Virkemidler til verdiskaping, innovasjon and mangfold på matområdet'

('Value Creation Programme for Food Production after 2010? Policy instruments for value creation, innovation and diversity in the food sector' – in Norwegian only) (p. 4), *regjeringen.no,* www.regjeringen. no/upload/LMD/Vedlegg/Brosjyrer_veiledere_rapporter/Rapport_ VSP_mat_etter_2010.pdf (read on 6 Jan. 2013).

41 Norwegian Food Safety Authority (2006) Internal document – *Notat om saksbehandlingen av sakene om BB (date: 13 March 2006, ref. 2004/ 7522).*

42 Proposition No 92 to the Storting (2000–2001), pp. 61–62.

43 As mentioned, this was again put on the agenda in 2008, when it was emphasised by Matmerk – the Norwegian Food Branding Foundation: Matmerk (2008) 'Lovbeskytter både industri- and håndverksproduksjon' ('Legal protection for both industrial and craft production' – in Norwegian only) *matmerk.no,* http://matmerk. no/nyhet/2008/lovbeskytter-bade-industri-and-handverksproduksjon (read on 13 July 2010).

44 Recommendation No 117 to the Odelsting (2000–2001).

45 Recommendation No 317 to the Storting (2000–2001), p. 7.

46 Deliberations in the Odelsting No 52 (2000–2001), case no 7.

47 Decision No 133 by the Odelsting, cf. Recommendation No 117 to the Odelsting (2000–2001) pertaining to Proposition No 85 to the Odelsting (2000–2001).

48 Kongshaug, L. I. (2002) 'Større mangfold av mat', *Bergens Tidende* 30 Sept. 2002.

49 Annual report of Matmerk – the Norwegian Food Branding Foundation for 2003 (p. 12).

50 Dagligvarehandelen (2004) 'Beskyttede betegnelser' ('Geographical indications' – in Norwegian only), *dagligvarehandelen.no,* www.dagligv arehandelen.no/xp/pub/hoved/avisen/tidligere_utg/22816 (read on 27 Sept. 2012).

51 Matmerk – Norske matmerker, *Årsmelding 2005: Mangfold and muligheter* ('Annual report 2005: Diversity and opportunities' – in Norwegian only) (p. 10).

52 Riis-Johansen, T. (2006) 'Næringsstrategi for fremtiden Beskyttede betegnelser' ('Business strategy for the future of the Norwegian PDO, PGI and TSG scheme' – in Norwegian only), *regjeringen.no,* www. regjeringen.no/nb/dep/lmd/aktuelt/taler_artikler/ministeren/tidligere_ landbruks_and_matminister_riis_/2006/naringsstrategi-for-fremtiden-beskyttede.html?id=430224 (read on 21 Aug. 2010).

53 For information about the status at the time of the Norwegian GI scheme's tenth anniversary, see Hegnes's op-ed article and Nina Sundqvist's response in the Norwegian newspaper *Nationen* on 5 and 12 July 2012, respectively.

54 Brekk, L. P. (2009) 'Lokal mat – nasjonale muligheter' ('Local food, national opportunities'), Norwegian regional newspaper *Adresseavisen* 13 February 2009.

55 A number of similar success stories are highlighted in *VSP mat etter 2010?* to legitimise further investment in speciality foods. Documents advocating the quality turn rarely mention all those who were unable to adapt to the new food culture and market.

56 Brekk, L. P. (2011) 'Fremtidens Mat-Norge' ('Food Norway of the future' – in Norwegian only), *regjeringen.no*, www.regjeringen.no/se/dep/lmd/aktuelt/taler_artikler/ministeren/landbruks--and-matminis ter-lars-peder-bre/2011/tale-fremtidens-mat-norge.html?id=630635 (read on 4 Nov. 2011).

57 Proposition No 133 to the Storting (2009-2010), pp. 65–66.

58 'VSP mat etter 2010? Virkemidler til verdiskaping, innovasjon and mangfold på matområdet' ('Value Creation Programme for Food Production after 2010? Policy instruments for value creation, innovation and diversity in the food sector' – in Norwegian only) (p. 4), *regjeringen.no*, www.regjeringen.no/upload/LMD/Vedlegg/ Brosjyrer_veiledere_rapporter/Rapport_VSP_mat_etter_2010.pdf (read on 6 Jan. 2013).

59 Excerpt from an interview with an administrator.

60 The Norwegian Food Branding Foundation (2008) 'Butikk-trening for lokalmatprodusenter' ('Shop training for local food producers'), *matmerk.no*, http://matmerk.no/nyhet/2008/butikk-trening-for-loka lmatprodusenter (read on 7 Jan. 2012).

61 The Norwegian Food Branding Foundation (2011) 'Høring av utkast til forskrift av *Prosciutto di Parma* som opprinnelsesbetegnelse' (ref. 5510/585, 21 Nov. 2011, pp. 1–2).

62 Knut Haukelid (2008) has described a similar situation involving local reindeer hunters and the Norwegian authorities and their knowledge and assessments of a local reindeer population. While the authorities believed that the population was sufficiently large to be hunted, local hunters believed that the number of animals had decreased and hunting should not be allowed. The controversy resulted, firstly, in the hunters going on 'strike' and, secondly, in the authorities adjusting their figures, which in turn resulted in an official hunting ban being introduced.

63 Another comment on this form of alienation is that it is linked to imma-terial rather than material production, although both are involved in the overall adaptation work. In a historical perspective, we can see a shift from alienation being associated with material production and transformations to being associated with immaterial production and translations.

64 Amended through regulations No 1281 of 24 October 2003, No 383 of 13 February 2004, No 300 of 19 March 2007, No 526 of 18 May 2007, No 1805 of 23 December 2009, No 1852 of 17 December 2010, and No 1417 of 19 December 2011.

65 Proposition No 85 to the Odelsting (2000-2001).

66 I understand discourse as *a particular way of talking about and understanding the world (or an aspect of the world)* (Jørgensen and Phillips 1999:9) that has social consequences.

67 My own inaccurate, but consistent, use of the term 'framework regulation' is intended as a reminder of the translation work that takes place when a common European system is adapted to Norway's legal and food culture.

68 FOR 2006-11-14 nr 1235: Regulations No 1235 of 14 November 2006 on the protection of 'Gamalost frå Vik' as a protected geographical indication, Section 3 third subsection.

69 Interview with a producer.

70 Framework regulation, Section 14.

71 Proposition No 85 to the Odelsting (2000–2001), p. 3.

72 Proposition No 85 to the Odelsting (2000–2001), p. 2.

73 FOR 2007-12-11 nr 1814: Regulation No 1814 of 11 December 2007 on the protection of 'Tørrfisk fra Lofoten' as a protected geographical indication, Section 3(3).

74 FOR 2006-10-27 nr 1196: Regulation No 1196 of 27 October 2006 on the protection of 'Rakfisk fra Valdres' as a protected geographical indication, Section 3(3).

75 FOR 2012-10-03 nr 935: Regulation No 935 of 3 October 2012 on the protection of 'Fenalår fra Norge' as a protected geographical indication of origin, Section 3(1).

76 Framework regulation, Section 9(2).

77 Framework regulations, Section 9(1).

78 See Hegnes (2012) for a more comprehensive review of adaptation work with particular reference to these potato varieties.

79 FOR 2006-05-26 nr 554: Regulations No 554 of 26 May 2006 on the protection of 'Fjellmandel fra Oppdal' as a protected geographical indication

80 Framework regulations, Section 9(7).

81 Recommendation No 117 to the Odelsting (2000–2001), p. 8.

82 The colours of the Norwegian logos from 2002 are blue and white. The colours of the EU logos from 1992 was blue and yellow. From 2008 the PDO logo in EU was changed to red and yellow.

83 *Only those to whom protection has been granted under the Regulations on PDO, PGI and TSG may use the logo and product designation protected pursuant to the specific product regulations. The designations and logos can also be used in the Nynorsk form of Norwegian, with the*

following wording: 'beskytta opphavsnemning', 'beskytta geografisk nemning' or 'beskytta tradisjonelt særpreg'. South Sami and North Sami versions of the designations and logo can also be used, but they must be used together with the Norwegian Bokmål or Norwegian Nynorsk version. See Section 4 of the Regulations on PDO, PGI and TSG. The logos for PDO, PGI and TSG are identical in design. It is the text in the logo that communicates which form of protection has been granted. The written designation and the logo should preferably be reproduced in blue and white, but may in certain cases also be approved in black and white. On packaging, the minimum size of the logo is 15 mm, while the minimum size for printed material has been set to 20 mm in diameter. The designation for which GI recognition has been granted must be used as the product/trade name. (The Norwegian Food Branding Foundation (undated) 'Retningslinjer for bruk av logoer and produktbetegnelser' ('Guidelines for the use of logos and product designations' – in Norwegian only), *beskyttedebetegnelser.no,* www.beskyttedebetegnel ser.no/for-produsenter/retningslinjer-bruk-av-logoer-and-produktbete gnelser/ (read on 24 November 2012).

84 Framework regulations, Section 9(3).
85 FOR 2004-06-01 nr 819: Regulations No 1196 of 1 June 2004 on the protection of the product designation 'Ringerikserter' as a protected designation of origin, Section 3(2).
86 COUNCIL REGULATION (EC) No 510/2006 of 20 March 2006 on the protection of geographical indications and designations of origin for agricultural products and foodstuffs.
87 In 2023 there are three products approved with Norway as the approved area.
88 FOR 2012-10-03 nr 935: Regulations No 935 of 3 October 2012 on the protection of 'Fenalår fra Norge' as a protected geographical indication of origin, Section 3(2).
89 FOR 2010-11-04 nr 1402: Regulations No 1402 of 4 November 2010 on the protection of 'Villsau frå Norskekysten' as a protected geographical indication, Section 3(2).
90 See Hegnes 2019 (based on this section) for a more elaborate analysis on adapting geographical boundaries for PDO and PGI in Norway.
91 Framework regulation, Section 9(5).
92 Framework regulations, Section 9(4).
93 The Norwegian Food Branding Foundation (Matmerk) and the Norwegian Quality System for Agriculture (KSL) merged with effect from 1 January 2007 to form the Norwegian Agricultural Quality System and Food Branding Foundation *(KSL Matmerk)*
94 Framework regulations, Section 9(6).
95 The arrangement of documents and letters is organised alphabetically within chronologically sorted two-year periods. Documents and letters

dated to only one specific year are placed at the end of the period to which they naturally belong. For example, a letter from 2004 would be placed at the end of the 2004-2005 period.
96 Pricing/valuation is a well-known adaptation practice in the field of economics. It also forms part of cultural adaptation work but is not an important point in the present analysis. However, it might be interesting to consider pricing in relation to other adaptation practices in subsequent analyses.

Research publications

Albayrak, M. and Gunes, E. (2010) 'Implementations of Geographical Indications at Brand Management of Traditional Foods in the European Union', *African Journal of Business Management*, 4: 1059–1068.

Amilien, V. and Hegnes, A. W. (2004) 'The Cultural Smell of Fermented Fish – About the Development of a Local Product in Norway', *Food, Agriculture & Environment*, 1: 141–147.

Amilien, V. and Hegnes, A. W. (2007) 'Mellom konserverende and innoverende: Om begrepet tradisjonsmat', in Amilien, V. and Krogh, E. (eds.) *Den kultiverte maten* (pp. 135–157) Bergen: Fagbokforlaget.

Amilien, V., Fort, F. and Ferras, N. (2007) 'Hyper-Real Territories and Urban Markets: Changing Conventions for Local Food – Case Studies from France and Norway', *Anthropology of Food*, http://aof.revues.org/446

Barham, E. (2003) 'Translating Terroir: The Global Challenge of French AOC labeling', *Journal of Rural Studies*, 19: 127–138.

Bérard, L. and Marchenay, P. (2008) *From Localized Products to Geographical Indications. Awareness and Action.* Bourg-en-Bresse: CNRS Ressources des terroirs.

Bilden, K. M. (2011) *Mat er makt: Myter and muligheter i matens storpolitikk.* Oslo: Aschehoug.

Bowen, S. (2011) 'The Importance of Place: Re-territorialising Embeddedness', *Sociologia Ruralis*, 51: 325–348.

Bowen, S. and De Master, K. (2011) 'New Rural Livelihoods or Museums of Production? Quality Food Initiatives in Practice', *Journal of Rural Studies*, 27: 73–82.

Bråten, S. (2000) *Modellmakt and altersentriske spedbarn.* Bergen: SIGMA.

Canãda, J. S. and Vázquez, A. M. (2005) 'Quality Certification, Institutions and Innovation in Local Agro-Food Systems: Protected Designations of Origin of Olive Oil in Spain', *Journal of Rural Studies*, 21: 475–486.

Cochoy, F. (2007) 'A Sociology of Market-Things: On Tending the Garden of Choices in Mass Retailing', *The Sociological Review*, 55: 109–129.

Connerton, P. (1989) *How Societies Remember*. Cambridge: Cambridge University Press.

Connerton, P. (2009) *How Modernity Forgets*. Cambridge: Cambridge University Press.

Ehn, B. and Löfgren, O. (2012) 'Pausens mikrodramatik – En essä om önskade och oönskade avbrott', *Sosiologi i dag*, 42: 15–36.

Goodman, D. (2004) 'Rural Europe Redux? Reflections on Alternative Agro-Food Networks and Paradigm Change', *Sociologia Ruralis*, 44: 3–16.

Haukelid K. (2008) *Hunters on Strike – Knowledge, Ethics and Aesthetics in Reindeer Hunting and Wildlife Management*. Paper to the ASA-conference 2008, University of Auckland, New Zealand.

Hegnes A.W. (2019) 'The Map and the Terroir: Adapting Geographical Boundaries for PDO and PGI in Norway', *British Food Journal* 121: 3024–3042.

Hegnes, A. W. (2007) 'Understanding the Temporal Ambiguity of Local Foods through "Polytemporality": The Case of Norwegian Gamalost fra Vik (Old Cheese)', *Anthropology of Food*, http://aof.rev ues.org/458.

Hegnes, A. W. (2012) 'Introducing and Practicing PDO and PGI in Norway – Turning to Protected Quality Through Translations of Meaning and Transformations of Materiality', *Anthropology of Food*, http://aof.revues.org/7210.

Hjortland, E. (2003) *Flaskehalser and etableringsbarrierer for mindre matbedrifter: En handlingsplan for å fremme nyskaping and få frem flere matbedrifter*. SND-rapport 2-2003. Oslo: Statens nærings – and distriktsutviklingsfond.

Hobsbawm, E. (1983) 'Introduction: Inventing Traditions', in Hobsbawm, E. and Ranger, T. (eds.) *The Invention of Tradition* (pp. 1–14). Cambridge: Cambridge University Press.

Jacobsen, E. (1999) *Produktutvikling and sortimentspolitikk i kjedenes tid? Noen betraktninger om "rimifiseringen" av mattilbudet i Norge*. Arbeidsnotat nr. 12. Lysaker: Statens institutt for forbruksforskning.

Jørgensen, M. W. and Phillips, L. (1999) *Diskursanalyse som teori and metode*. Frederiksberg: Roskilde Universitetsforlag.

Lie, A. and Veggeland, F. (2010) *Globalisering and matpolitikk. Flernivåstyring – WTO, EU and Norge*. Oslo: Universitetsforlaget.

Muchnik, J., Biénabe, E. and Cerdan, C. (2005) 'Food Identity/Food Quality: Insights from the "Coalho" Cheese in the Northeast of Brazil', *Anthropology of Food*, http://aof.revues.org/110?&id=110.

Nygård, B. and Storstad, O. (1998) 'De-Globalization of Food Markets? Consumer Perceptions of Safe Food: The Case of Norway', *Sociologia Ruralis*, 38: 35–53.

Østerberg, D. (1998) *Arkitektur and sosiologi i Oslo – en sosio-materiell fortolkning*. Oslo: Pax.

Parrott, N., Wilson, N. and Murdoch, J. (2002) 'Spatializing Quality: Regional Protection and the Alternative Geography of Food', *European Urban and Regional Studies*, 9: 241–261.

Paxon, H. (2010) 'Locating Value in Artisan Cheese: Reverse Engineering *Terroir* for New-World Landscapes', *American Anthropologist*, 112: 444–457.

Rem, S. (2008) 'Å stemme med gaffelen: Vendingen mot forbrukerne i norsk matpolitikk', in Asdal, K. and Moser, I. (eds.) *Ekspertise and brukermakt* (pp. 41–67). Oslo: Unipub.

Rommetvedt, H. (2002) *Matmakt: Politikk, forhandling, marked*. Bergen: Fagbokforlaget.

Rosati, M. (2009) *QUALIGEO: Atlas of European and Non-European PDO, PGI, TSG agri-food products*. Siena: Fondazione Qualivita.

Rusaanes, Å. M. H. and Hjortland, E. (2000) *Handlingsplan for norsk matkultur: Norge på menyen*. SND-rapport nr 1-2000. Oslo: SND.

Tregear, A., Arfini, F., Belletti, G. and Marescotti, A. (2007) 'Regional Foods and Rural Development: The Role of Product Qualification', *Journal of Rural Studies*, 23: 12–22.

Weber, M. (1978) *Economy and Society: An Outline of Interpretive Sociology*. Berkeley, California: University of California Press.

Wittgenstein, L. (2001) *Philosophical Investigations: The German Text, with a Revised English Translation*. Oxford: Blackwell.

Official documents

1988–1989

St.prp. nr. 128 (1988–89) Jordbruksoppgjøret 1989 – Endringer i statsbudsjettet for 1989 and revidert budsjett for Statens Kornforretning m.m.

1989–1990

Innst. S. nr. 253 (1989–1990) Jordbruksoppgjøret 1990 – Endringer i statsbudsjettet for 1990 and revidert budsjett for Statens Kornforretning m.m.

St.prp. nr. 112 (1989–1990) Jordbruksoppgjøret 1990 – Endringer i statsbudsjettet for 1990 and revidert budsjett for Statens Kornforretning m.m.

1990–1991

NOU 1991:2B, Norsk landbrukspolitikk – Utfordringer, mål and virkemidler, Hovedinnstilling.
St.prp. nr. 1. Tillegg nr. 1 (1990–1991) Om endring av St.prp. nr. 1 om statsbudsjettet medregnet folketrygden for 1991.

1992–1993

Landbruksdepartementet (1992) *Konkurransestrategier for norsk mat (Ren Mat-strategien)*.
St.prp. nr. 8 (1992–1993) Landbruk i utvikling – Om retningslinjer for landbrukspolitikken and opplegget for jordbruksoppgjørene m.v.

1996–1997

NOU 1996:10 – Effektiv matsikkerhet.
St.meld. nr. 40 (1996–1997) Matkvalitet and forbrukertrygghet.

1999–2000

Innst. S. nr. 167 (1999–2000) Innstilling fra næringskomiteen om norsk landbruk and matproduksjon – St.meld. nr. 19 (1999–2000).
St.meld. nr. 19 (1999–2000) Om norsk landbruk and matproduksjon.
St.prp. nr. 82 (1999–2000) Om jordbruksoppgjøret 2000 – endringer i statsbudsjettet for 2000 m.m.
Stiftelsen Godt Norsk (1999). Årsmelding.

2000–2001

Besl. O. nr. 133 Jf. Innst. O. nr. 117 (2000–2001) (7. juni 2001) and Ot.prp. nr. 85 (2000–2001).
Dokument nr. 8:96 (2000–2001) Forslag fra stortingsrepresentantene Terje Johansen and Leif Helge Kongshaug om samkjøring av ressurser til styrking av norsk matvaresikkerhet and utvikling av norske konkurransedyktige landbruksprodukter av høy kvalitet.
Forhandlinger i Odelstinget nr. 52 (2000–2001) Sak nr. 7. Innstilling fra næringskomiteen om lov om endringer i lov 17. juni 1932 nr. 6 om kvalitetskontroll med landbruksvarer m.v. (Hjemmel for norsk merkeordning for landbruksprodukter) (Innst. O. nr. 117 (2000–2001), jf. Ot.prp. nr. 85 (2000–2001).
Innst. O. nr. 117 (2000–2001) Innstilling fra næringskomiteen om lov om endringer i lov 17. juni 1932 nr. 6 om kvalitetskontroll

med landbruksvarer m.v. (Hjemmel for norsk merkeordning for landbruksprodukter) Ot.prp. nr. 85 (2000–2001).

Innst. S. nr. 270 (2000–2001) Innstilling fra næringskomiteen om forslag fra stortingsrepresentantene Terje Johansen and Leif Helge Kongshaug om samkjøring av ressurser til styrking av norsk matvaresikkerhet and utvikling av norske konkurransedyktige landbruksprodukter av høy kvalitet. Dokument nr. 8:96 (2000–2001).

Innst. S. nr. 317 (2000–2001) Innstilling fra næringskomiteen om reindriftsavtalen 2001–2002, om dekning av kostnader vedrørende radioaktivitet i reinkjøtt, and om endringer i statsbudsjettet for 2001. St.prp. nr. 70 (2000–2001).

Landbruksdepartementet (2000) Høringsbrev ref. 99/02486. Dato: 2000-12-21.

Ot.prp. nr. 85 (2000–2001) Om lov om endringer i lov 17. juni 1932 nr. 6 om kvalitetskontroll med landbruksvarer m.v. (Hjemmel for norsk merkeordning for landbruksprodukter).

St.prp. nr. 92 (2000–2001) Om jordbruksoppgjøret 2001 – endringer i statsbudsjettet for 2001 m.m.

2001–2002

Verdiskapingsprogrammet for matproduksjon – Et program for innovasjon and mangfold på matområdet (2001).

2002–2003

Matmerk – Norske matmerker, *Årsmelding 2003: Muligheter og merverdi*

2005–2006

Matmerk – Norske matmerker, *Årsmelding 2005: Mangfold and muligheter*.

Sponheim, L. (2005) 'Trender and utvikling av mat sett fra et politisk miljø. Innlegg på Brimi-konferansen', Lom, 21. september 2005.

Mattilsynet (2005) *Tilsynsmodell for mindre matbedrifter: Prosjektrapport og Tilsynsveiledere*

2006–2007

Matmerk – norske matmerker, *Aktivitetsrapport 2006.*

Mattilsynet (2006) Internt dokument – *Notat om saksbehandlingen av sakene om BB (dato: 13.3.2006 ref. 2004/7522).*

2009–2010

Prop. 133 S (2009–2010) Proposisjon til Stortinget (forslag til stortingsvedtak) Jordbruksoppgjøret 2010 – endringer i statsbudsjettet for 2010 m.m.

2010–2011

NOU 2011:4, *Mat, makt and avmakt – om styrkeforholdene i verdikjeden for mat.*

2011–2012

Matmerk (2011) Høring av utkast til forskrift av *Prosciutto di Parma* som opprinnelsesbetegnelse (ref. 5510/585, 21.11.2011).

Newspaper articles

Aftenposten (2009) 'Eksklusivt matmerke helt ukjent'. Nyheter s. 7, 24.06.2009.
Aftenposten (2012) 'Merket mat til å stole på'. Innsikt s. 12, 11.10.2012.
Brekk, L. P. (2009) 'Lokal mat – nasjonale muligheter', *Adresseavisen* 13.02.09.
Hegnes, A. W. (2012) 'Ti års tilpasningsarbeid', *Nationen* 5.7.12.
Kongshaug, L. I. (2002) 'Større mangfold av mat', *Bergens Tidende* 30.09.02.
Sundqvist, N. (2012) '10-åring med ambisjoner', *Nationen* 12.7.2012.

Internet

Arbeiderpartiet, Sosialistisk Venstreparti and Senterpartiet (2005) 'Plattform for regjeringssamarbeidet mellom Arbeiderpartiet, Sosialistisk Venstreparti and Senterpartiet, 2005–09', *regjeringen.no,* www.regjeringen.no/upload/SMK/Vedlegg/2005/regjeringsplatform_ SoriaMoria.pdf (Accessed 6.1.2013).
Arbeiderpartiet, Sosialistisk Venstreparti and Senterpartiet (2009) 'Politisk plattform for flertallsregjeringen utgått av Arbeiderpartiet, Sosialistisk Venstreparti and Senterpartiet, 2009–2013, *regjeringen.no*, www.regjeringen.no/upload/SMK/Vedlegg/2009/Ny_politisk_plattfo rm_2009-2013.pdf (Accessed 6.1.2013).
Brekk, L. P. (2011) 'Fremtidens Mat-Norge', *regjeringen.no,* www.regjerin gen.no/se/dep/lmd/aktuelt/taler_artikler/ministeren/landbruks--and-matminister-lars-peder-bre/2011/tale-fremtidens-mat-norge.html?id= 630635 (Accessed 4.10.2011).

116   The food-cultural adaptation work of Norwegian GIs

Brekk, L. P. (2009) 'Tale for Norsk sau and geit – Fagorganisasjonen for sau – and geiteholdere', *regjeringen.no*, www.regjeringen.no/nb/dep/lmd/aktuelt/taler_artikler/ministeren/landbruks--and-matminister-lars-peder-bre/2009/innlegg-mote-hos-norsk-sau-and-geit-.html?id=573325 (Accessed 19.10.2010).

Commission of the European Communities (2008) 'Green paper on agricultural product quality: Product standards, farming requirements and quality schemes' (s. 15), *europa.eu*, http://eur-lex.europa.eu/LexUriServ/LexUriServ.do?uri=COM:2008:0641:FIN:EN:PDF (Accessed 7.1.2012).

Dagligvarehandelen (2004) 'Beskyttede betegnelser', *dagligvarehandelen. no*, www.dagligvarehandelen.no/xp/pub/hoved/avisen/tidligere_utg/22816 (Accessed 27.9.2012).

European Commission – Directorate-General for Agriculture and Rural Development (2009) 'Conclusions from the consultation on agricultural product quality' (s. 15), *europa.eu*, http://ec.europa.eu/agriculture/quality/policy/consultation/contributions/summary_en.pdf (Accessed 7.1.2012).

Fiskeridepartementet, Helsedepartementet, Landbruksdepartementet, i samarbeid med Barne – and familiedepartementet (2004) 'Handlingsplan for forbrukerretting av matpolitikken 2004–2005', *regjeringen.no*, www.regjeringen.no/upload/kilde/ld/rap/2004/0003/ddd/pdfv/209925-handlingsplan_mat_110504.pdf (Accessed 20.10.2010).

Landbruks – and matdepartementet (2005) 'Mat: Lettere å starte småskalaproduksjon', *regjeringen.no*, www.regjeringen.no/nb/dokumentarkiv/Regjeringen-Bondevik-II/Landbruks--and-matdepartementet/233194/2005/mat-lettere_a_starte_smaskalaproduksjon.html?id=258179 (Accessed 12.09.2011).

Landbruks – and matdepartementet (2010) 'VSP mat etter 2010? Virkemidler til verdiskaping, innovasjon and mangfold på matområdet', *regjeringen.no*, www.regjeringen.no/upload/LMD/Vedlegg/Brosjyrer_veiledere_rapporter/Rapport_VSP_mat_etter_2010.pdf (Accessed 6.1.2013).

Landbruksdepartementet (2000) 'Opprinnelsesmerking (AOC) i Frankrike – Rapport fra studietur 27.–30. juni 2000', *regjeringen.no*, www.regjeringen.no/nb/dep/lmd/dok/rapporter-and-planer/rapporter/2000/opprinnelsesmerking-aoc-i-frankrike-.html?id=277351 (Accessed 20.10.2010).

Matmerk (2008) 'Butikk-trening for lokalmatprodusenter', *matmerk.no*, http://matmerk.no/nyhet/2008/butikk-trening-for-lokalmatprodusenter (Accessed 7.1.2012).

Matmerk (2008) 'Lovbeskytter både industri – and håndverksproduksjon', *matmerk.no*, http://matmerk.no/nyhet/2008/lovbeskytter-bade-industri-and-handverksproduksjon (Accessed 13.7.2010).

Matmerk (udat.) 'Retningslinjer for bruk av logoer and produktbetegnelser', *beskyttedebetegnelser.no*, www.beskyttedebetegnelser.no/for-produsen ter/retningslinjer-bruk-av-logoer-and-produktbetegnelser/ (Accessed 24.11.2012).

Riis-Johansen, T. (2006) 'Næringsstrategi for fremtiden Beskyttede betegnelser', *regeringen.no*, www.regjeringen.no/nb/dep/lmd/aktuelt/ taler_artikler/ministeren/tidligere_landbruks_and_matminister_ri is_/2006/naringsstrategi-for-fremtiden-beskyttede.html?id=430224 (Accessed 21.8.2010).

Regulations

FOR 2002-07-05 nr 698: Forskrift om beskyttelse av opprinnelsesbetegnelser, geografiske betegnelser and betegnelser for tradisjonelt særpreg på næringsmidler

Forskrift om endring i forskrift om beskyttelse av opprinnelsesbetegnelser, geografiske betegnelser and betegnelser for tradisjonelt særpreg på landbruksbaserte næringsmidler: FOR-2003-10-24-1281, FOR-2004-02-13-383, FOR-2007-03-19-300, FOR-2007-05-18-526, FOR-2009-12-23-1805, FOR-2010-12-17-1852, FOR-2011-12-19-1417

FOR 2004-06-01 nr 819: Forskrift om beskyttelse av produktbetegnelsen Ringerikserter som Beskyttet opprinnelsesbetegnelse

FOR 2006-05-26 nr 554: Forskrift om beskyttelse av produktbetegnelsen Fjellmandel fra Oppdal som Beskyttet geografisk betegnelse

FOR 2006-10-27 nr 1196: Forskrift om beskyttelse av produktbetegnelsen Rakfisk fra Valdres som Beskyttet geografisk betegnelse

FOR 2006-11-14 nr 1235: Forskrift om vern av produktnemninga Gamalost frå Vik som beskytta geografisk nemning

FOR 2007-12-11 nr 1814: Forskrift om beskyttelse av Tørrfisk fra Lofoten som geografisk betegnelse

FOR 2010-11-04 nr 1402: Forskrift om vern av Villsau frå Norskekysten som geografisk nemning

FOR 2012-10-03 nr 935: Forskrift om beskyttelse av Fenalår fra Norge som geografisk betegnelse

COUNCIL REGULATION (EC) No 510/2006 of 20 March 2006 on the protection of geographical indications and designations of origin for agricultural products and foodstuffs

3 Conclusions

Through the empirical material I have described in three sub-analyses how the scheme for PDO, PGI, and TSG was prepared and subsequently administered and used in Norway and how cultural adaptation work is a recurring feature of all these phases. The three phases have more specifically been characterised by translations, reorganisations, and transformations, as well as numerous other adaptation practices and the interaction between them. The different adaptation practices have played different roles in the different sub-analyses. Reorganisations and particularly translations were important during the preparations and implementation phase. Reorganisations and translations still play an important role in the scheme's administration but are now on a somewhat more equal footing than during the preparatory phase. The producers using the scheme appear to engage in the most extensive form of adaptation work, which requires both translations, reorganisations, and transformations. Some adaptation practices are less frequently used than others, but nevertheless contribute to the overall adaptation work that the Norwegian system of GIs relies on in order to function.

The identification and development of the conceptual framework of cultural adaptation work gives, at least, three conceptual implications: Firstly, the system of concepts can be transferred and further developed in studies of similar schemes in other countries and food cultures. In such studies new adaptive practices can be identified, in addition to the main practices and the already less mentioned common practices in the Norwegian example, such as *rewriting, sorting, localisations,* and *re-localisations.* The practices

DOI: 10.4324/9781003143024-3

that are less common in this study could play a more important role in other studies, while some of the practices that play a key role in the Norwegian example may be less relevant somewhere else. New studies can contribute to nuance the understanding of the extensive and complex adaptation work that takes place when implementing GIs. In the long term, these practices can form important elements in a more developed conceptual toolbox. Secondly, cultural adaptation work is an appropriate point of departure for further developing and streamlining the understanding of previously identified adaptations more generally. Thirdly, the conceptual framework can relate constructively in the development of other theories of social science (e.g., social practice theory).

The analysis shows how the adaptations unfold and how its various consequences contribute to the scheme having an ambiguous influence on development of Norwegian GIs and Norwegian food culture. The consequences are, to varying degrees, in line with the aims of the scheme. The analysis shows how the adaptation work brings with it a new vocabulary and new food-cultural knowledge. This makes it possible to communicate and understand links between food, people, and place, which have previously not been emphasised in Norwegian food culture. Hence, the new vocabulary and understanding are in line with the scheme's aims of preserving important knowledge about Norwegian food and food culture. It appears, however, that the adaptation work also promotes innovation and sometimes alienates producers from their own products in the course of the application process, which conflicts with the aim of preserving knowledge. The adaptation work also includes adjustment of product names, and the demarcation of geographic origin moves from being determined by valleys and other natural boundaries, to being defined based on municipal boundaries. This is consistent, to varying degrees, with the intention of giving sufficient information to consumers and preserving important knowledge about Norwegian food and food culture. Another consequence of the adaptation work is that it plays a part in products becoming more similar, which again results in fewer product types. This also conflicts with the scheme's aim of contributing to increased variety of foodstuffs. As a whole, the scheme is often described as being modelled according to the European system. However, if one views the scheme as a consequence of the adaptation work, it appears to be a tailor-made Norwegian model with European profile. Identification of the adaptation work and its consequences also has political implications. The scheme is balanced, between being a political tool for developing Norwegian food production and value-adding. At the same time, as from a legal perspective, it is associated with the corresponding body of law and the scheme in the EU. If the scheme is excessively adapted to the Norwegian context, it may risk losing its credibility and validity in the EU. If it is excessively adapted to the European scheme, it may be perceived as cumbersome and meaningless for Norwegian producers, retailers, and consumers. The considerations and priorities of adaptations made by politicians will have consequences for the development of the scheme. Hence, knowledge of the cultural adaptation work of PDO, PGI and TSG can contribute to a better political and administrational foundation for governing the scheme, and what function it should have in the future.

4 Postscript

The sustainable turn and the future of geographical indications

In recent years there have been several calls for transforming the global food systems to improve health and food security and mitigate climate change. Recently, the European Green Deal, and more specifically the Farm to Fork Strategy (F2F), stresses the importance of sustainable practices in all sectors and levels of the food chain. Accompanying this strengthened sustainable turn is an increased attention to sustainability certification in the agrifood sector, with a multitude of already existing schemes with various criteria. The number of schemes and the complexity of standards represents a challenge with respect to which sustainability objectives are targeted. A consequence of this complexity is a parallel demand for simplification and harmonisation of standards. In an ideal situation, e.g., from the supplier's point of view, one would only need to comply with one set of criteria to meet all government and proprietor-based standards (Richards et al. 2013:238).

Towards a sustainable food nation

In Norway, sustainability is an integrated feature of several private and governmental certification schemes for food. To meet the need for a safe and sustainable food system, Norwegian governmental authorities have recently initiated various political initiatives. One of them is the the "Matnasjonen Norge" (Food Nation Norway), which was launched in 2021. This cross-sectoral strategy provides a political framework for positioning Norway as a 'Food Nation' globally by 2030. Based on the UN Sustainable Development Goals, the strategy envisions that, by 2030, food will be a source

DOI: 10.4324/9781003143024-4

of joy, pride, good health, and bonding among the population, and will also serve as a prominent element in Norway's tourism industry. GIs are particularly connected to the development of food tourism in the strategy. This initiative of relating GIs to tourism in Norwegian food culture is taking place at the same time as sustainability measures are being increasingly emphasised within the international discussions on the GI system. However, it is left unclear how Norwegian GIs can contribute to this sustainable turn. To understand this 'blind spot' in the Norwegian strategies for GIs a recap of the history on how Norwegian food labelling schemes have been related to sustainable measures, and especially the environmental aspect, may contribute to clarification.

Sustainability and Norwegian cannibal food schemes

Different notions of sustainability have motivated the development of Norwegian food labelling schemes since the late 1980s. A historical timeline of Norwegian food labelling/certification can be drawn, commencing in 1986 with a 'green wave' representing the introduction of the scheme for organic quality in Norway. Some of the schemes have developed from private initiatives and later been implemented in official regulatory framework, as was also the case for the scheme for organic food.

The development and institutionalisation of the organic quality was initiated by farmers and can be traced back to bio-dynamic agriculture in the 1930s as an alternative movement, inspired by the Rudolf Steiner philosophy (Amilien et al. 2008:47). This pioneer group of farmers was later accompanied with stakeholders who had focus on the environmental aspects arguing that conventional agriculture was developing in the wrong direction according to environmental considerations, such as becoming more dependent of fertilisers and pesticides. The Norwegian control and certification body (Debio) was established in 1986, initiated by organic farmers. Debio was established because the organic producers had no legal protection, and they experienced that some producers labelled their products as organic without being organic. First, a private law standard that was voluntary to associate with was established. Then, after 1992, Norwegian organic products had to comply with EU regulations to be classified as organic.

Towards the end of the 1980s, global and European trade policies were undergoing major changes. General increased liberalisation and import tax deregulation threatened Norwegian food products with increased competition from imports. To counter the competition, Norwegian authorities and other key agri-food stakeholders started mobilising what became to be described as *mental border protection* (Hegnes and Amilien 2019). Simply put, the strategy aimed to trigger new ways of thinking about and looking at food and to convince Norwegian consumers to choose Norwegian products, as also mentioned in the introductions chapter.

The green wave was later followed by a focus on national quality and the introduction of the 'Good Norwegian' scheme in 1994, indicating compliance with a standardised level of quality for Norwegian food. In a speech held by the Minister agriculture in 1991, Gunhild Øyangen, advantages explicitly mentioned were clean food from Norway and regional or "special Norwegian" products that are industrially processed, for example aquavit (Øyangen 1991:8). New schemes were introduced as combined tools for protecting the Norwegian market from international economic competition and at the same time protect consumers from health-related risk represented by the same imported foodstuff. The label scheme "Godt Norsk" was triggered by, and a counterpart to, the emerging globalised trade cooperation. "Godt Norsk" derived its meaning and legitimacy through a more or less explicit claim that Norwegian products are safe, while there are various forms of risk associated with agricultural products coming from abroad (Hegnes 2015:226).

The Norwegian top-down *turn to new qualities* coincided with a growing focus on new qualities in Europe characterised by a bottom-up initiative by consumers, retailers and producers away from standardised products towards alternative qualities (Goodman 2003). Both the top-down and bottom-up initiatives may be understood as nuances of *gastronationalism,* as described by DeSoucey (2010).

To raise awareness of Norwegian food specialties, attempts were made to develop a new food vocabulary and mentality through the introduction of a new food cultural taxonomy. The focus on food specialties became more explicit, with several Ministers of Food and Agriculture using France and southern Europe as ideal examples for how this model benefits those countries. Since the 1990s, the political opinion in Norway has in general been united in the belief that the domestic application of the concept of terroir will alter Norwegians' understanding of Norwegian food products. This desire to embrace terroir on a conceptual level, to communicate both Norway's history and build an exciting food culture for its future, was stated by former Minister of Food and Agriculture, Lars Sponheim:

> We must develop and communicate the story of the Norwegian food production and to a much greater extent do as the French people. We must link food production to what is known as "terroir" in France, i.e. the indigenous, the identity making and specificity of soil and place.
>
> (Sponheim 2005)

The regional, local, traditional, and special qualities were first emphasised through the scheme "Specialty" in 2001. In July 2002, the Norwegian regulations for Geographical Indications entered into force in accordance with EU regulations.

Since the late 1980s it has been an ambition for The Norwegian Agricultural Authority (NAA) to increase the production and consumption of organic food in Norway. However, the last governments have had different ambitions about organic production and consumption. The targets have previously been 15 per cent organic food production and consumption by 2015,[1] and 15 per cent by 2020.[2] The seated government's goal is to *Stimulate increased production and sales of local food and drinks and organic food.*[3] Yet, the desired evolution has shown to be a long and winding road. In 2023 NAA reported that the market shares for organic food in 2022 was accounting for just under 2 per cent of the total sale of food and beverage products in Norway.[4]

The lack of demand for organic products has partly been ascribed to the notion that the Norwegian consumers understand conventional products as having similar qualities as organic (Storstad and Bjørkhaug 2003; Vittersø and Tangeland 2015). This exemplifies that national and international labeling schemes 'competes' in covering different qualities and the Norwegian contexts may be described as an arena of labelling cannibalisation, inspired by the concept of brand cannibalisation (*The extent to which one brand gains recognition and esteem at the expense of other similar brands from the same company).*[5] More specifically one may hypothesise that whereas the Godt norsk label may have gained recognition and esteem at the expense of the organic label, the label for Speciality may have gained recognition and esteem at the expense of GIs.

In recent years, new labelling initiatives with an environmental sustainability profile have emerged,[6] representing a shift from protecting humans from nature to protecting nature from humans. In sum, the different Norwegian schemes cover different aspects of SDG, as we know them today. Whereas the schemes for organic, biodynamic and recent certification initiatives relates to environmental and ecological aspects, Nyt Norge, Speciality and Geographical indications relates more to economic, social and food cultural aspects.

When quality labels cannibalise and receive little attention in producers and consumers' food practices 20 years after they were introduced, it is uncertain what kind of role GIs will play in Norway in the future. One can therefore ask if an increasing attention to sustainability will lead the way or if it will devaluate the future development of Norwegian GIs.

Sustainability and GIs

Despite a largely shared understanding of the crucial need for a sustainable turn, sustainability is still a multidimensional concept encompassing several matters and interests. During the last decade, a vast number of studies and various publications have offered detailed accounts of how GIs are related to various dimensions of sustainability, including environmental (e.g., Owen et al. 2020), economic (e.g., Vandecandelaere et al. 2020), social (e.g., Muller et al. 2021), and in combination (Bellassen et al. 2022; FAO 2023a; FAO 2023b). There are also specific examples of analysis of the Norwegian scheme from a sustainability perspective (Amilien et al. 2019).

Geographical indications relation to environmental sustainability can be positive and negative. GIs can contribute to preservation of biodiversity and traditional farming practices and production methods that are often more environmentally friendly. However, GIs can also encourage the intensification of production to meet growing demand, which may negatively impact the environment. This could include increased use of water, energy, and other resources, as well as potential over-exploitation of natural resources. GIs may also inadvertently promote standardisation and monoculture, as farmers and producers focus on a single crop or product associated with the GI. Overall, the relationship between geographical indications and environmental sustainability is complex and can depend on various factors, such as the specific product, region, and production practices. Encouraging responsible use and adaptations of GIs and supporting sustainable practices among producers can help maximise the positive impacts and minimise potential negative consequences.

Despite the fact that environmental sustainability has arisen to be an explicit and important quality in GIs and as an object of research during the last decade, environmental sustainability has hitherto been relatively absent, or implicit, in the discourse and Norwegian model for GIs. However, inspired by the ongoing revision in the EU for voluntary inclusion by the GI producer group of sustainability criteria in the product specification,[7] there are signals that the Norwegian scheme might also be directed to include sustainability measures in near future. This 'new' situation and sustainable turn internationally and in Norway triggers a need to explore and shed light on the debate on GIs *versus* sustainability standards. This debate is characterised by balancing advantages and drawbacks of at least two challenging strategies. The first strategy being a convergence strategy, implying inclusion of sustainability measures in GI certification, and the second being a distinction strategy, focusing GI certification on place-based specificity on one hand and sustainability standards on the other. The two alternative strategies can give different outcomes in the Norwegian context, depending on the strategies being strong or weak. A strong focus on place-based specificity, not including sustainability, may give increased attention to terroir qualities. However, the Norwegian history so far, show that this has been challenging. Balancing place-based specificity with sustainability measures may therefore, on the one hand, decrease the attention to the place-based specificity in GIs. However, it may also contribute to an increased attention to the scheme in total. The development of GIs in Norway will anyhow depend on several factors, such as the impact from EU and consumer and producer preferences.

Even though there have been recent advances in describing and understanding GIs from a sustainability perspective, there are still important questions associated with how people generally understand and adapt their GI practices to sustainable measures. This should motivate to ask several questions, such as: How do different actors understand, practice, and adapt the nexus of place-based specificity and sustainability qualities in GIs, and what consequences does this dynamic bring? Is a system of GIs for food in a food culture like the Norwegian ready to also include sustainability measures as discussed for the European model? Will it be easier to combine GIs with sustainable measures in food cultures with a weaker conception of terroir than in countries with a strong conception?

Obviously, there are strong arguments for including sustainability measures in the Norwegian system for GIs for foodstuff. However, as I have described, there are also arguments that do not point in that direction. Anyhow, the dualistic and general discussions on whether to include such measures or not need to be understood context specific on levels ranging from food cultures and specific GIs. This potential sustainable turn might also put the Norwegian GIs in a wider framework that might include new translations, reorganisations, and transformations, in addition to new adaptive practices that was not part of or not prominent in the first turn to quality.

Terroir incognita

Strongly related to the sustainable turn, new adaptive practices will also need to be addressed in a new and ongoing parallel third turn, concerning how artificial intelligence and associated technologies will impact on GIs and the accompanying research. In the textbox below I have recited the answer I got asking ChatGPT-4: *How will the system of Geographical Indications for food and drinks be influenced by artificial intelligence?*

Artificial intelligence (AI) will influence the system of Geographical Indications (GIs) for food and drinks in several ways:

1. Monitoring and enforcement: AI can help monitor and enforce GI protection by scanning online marketplaces,

social media, and other digital platforms for unauthorised use of GIs. Machine learning algorithms can analyse large datasets to identify potential infringements, enabling authorities to take appropriate actions more efficiently.

2. Authentication and quality control: AI technologies, such as machine learning and computer vision, can be used to authenticate GI food and drink products and ensure they meet required quality standards. AI could be trained to recognise specific sensory characteristics (e.g., color, aroma, taste) associated with GI food and drink products, helping to detect counterfeit items or unauthorised uses of the GI.

3. Supply chain management and traceability: AI can improve the traceability of GI food and drink products by monitoring and analysing data along the supply chain, from production to consumption. This can help guarantee the quality and authenticity of GI food and drink products, as well as provide valuable insights into consumer preferences and market trends. Blockchain technology, combined with AI, could further enhance traceability and transparency in the GI food and drink supply chain.

4. Consumer engagement and marketing: AI-powered marketing tools, such as chatbots, recommendation engines, and targeted advertising, can help producers of GI food and drink products better understand consumer preferences, reach a wider audience, and create more effective marketing strategies. AI can also be used to develop personalised recommendations for consumers based on their preferences, making it easier for them to discover and engage with GI food and drink products.

5. Legal and regulatory challenges: As AI continues to evolve, it may raise legal and regulatory challenges for the GI system. For example, AI-generated content or inventions could create uncertainty around ownership and protection of intellectual property rights, including GIs. Additionally, AI might be used to generate convincing counterfeits, posing challenges to GI enforcement and protection.

In conclusion, AI is likely to have significant implications for the GI system for food and drinks, including monitoring and enforcement, authentication and quality control, supply chain management and traceability, consumer engagement and marketing, and legal and regulatory challenges. As AI technologies continue to advance, stakeholders in the GI system will need to adapt and leverage these technologies to better protect and promote geographical indications for food and drink products.

Textbox 1.[8]

At first glance, the AI-answer seem to focus as much on the protection of the GI system as for the GI system protecting products, producers and consumers. However, it also indicates that the food cultures and their adaptation work will continue to be crucial.

Whereas the Norwegian quality turn was characterised by adapting GI to a Norwegian food culture lacking an understanding of the nexus of food, people and places, the ongoing, new and future turns will need adaptive practices to adapt Norwegian GIs to a new Norwegian food culture with a stronger emphasis on the quality of sustainability and new technologies. In combination with the evolution of consumer preferences, these turns calls for complex practical-conceptual and methodological tools to understand what role and functions GIs will have in this new food cultural context and evolution.

Notes

1 www.regjeringen.no/globalassets/upload/smk/vedlegg/2005/regjerings platform_soriamoria.pdf
2 www.regjeringen.no/globalassets/upload/smk/vedlegg/2009/ny_politisk _plattform_2009-2013.pdf
3 www.regjeringen.no/contentassets/cb0adb6c6fee428caa81bd5b33950 1b0/no/pdfs/hurdalsplattformen.pdf
4 www.landbruksdirektoratet.no/nb/nyhetsrom/nyhetsarkiv/salg-av-okologisk-mat-svakt-synkende
5 www.oxfordreference.com/display/10.1093/oi/authority.2011080309 5524428;jsessionid=0DA736F4157013FCC451C3483036CBDD
6 Examples on such certifications is the TORO Klimamerke (introduced in 2019) and a new animal welfare scheme (introduced in 2018) initiated by The Norwegian Animal Protection Alliance.

7 https://eur-lex.europa.eu/legal-content/EN/TXT/PDF/?uri=
CELEX:52022PC0134R(01)&from=EN
8 https://chat.openai.com/chat?model=gpt-4 (Accessed April 7th 2023).

Research literature and other sources

Research publications

Amilien, V., Schjøll, A. and Vramo, L. M. (2008) *Consumers Understanding Of Local Food* (Professional report no. 1). Torshov: SIFO (in Norwegian only). *Forbrukernes forståelse av lokal mat* (Fagrapport no. 1). Torshov: SIFO.

Amilien, V., Vittersø, G. and Tangeland, T. (2019) PGI Lofoten Stockfish in Norway. in: F. Arfini, F. and Bellassen, V. (eds.) *Sustainability of European Food Quality Schemes: Multi-Performance, Structure, and Governance of PDO, PGI, and Organic Agri-Food Systems* (pp. 507–527). Cham: Springer Nature.

Bellassen, V., Drut, M., Hilal, M., Bodini, A., Donati, M., Duboys de Labarre, M., Filipović, J., Gauvrit, L., Gil, J. M., Hoang, V., Malak-Rawlikowska, A., Mattas, K., Monier-Dilhan, S., Muller, P., Napasintuwong, O., Peerlings, J., Poméon, T., Maksan, M. T., Töröko, Á., Veneziani, M., Vittersø, G. and Arfini, F. (2022) 'The Economic, Environmental and Social Performance of European Certified Food', *Ecological Economics*, vol. 191, Article 107244.

DeSoucey, M. (2010) 'Gastronationalism: Food Traditions and Authenticity Politics in the European Union', *American Sociological Review*, 75: 432–455.

FAO (2023a) *Using Geographical Indications to Improve Sustainability – Lessons Learned from 15 Years of FAO Work on Geographical Indications*. Rome.

FAO (2023b) *Promoting Sustainability through the Registration of Geographical Indications – Guidelines for Public Authorities to Examine Applications*. Rome.

Goodman, D. (2003) 'The Quality "Turn" and Alternative Food Practices: Reflections and Agenda', *Journal of Rural Studies*, 19: 1–7.

Hegnes, A. W. (2015) 'Mentalt grensevern for norske landbruksprodukter: Tilpasningsarbeid i tre akter', in Bjørkhaug, H., Almås, R., Vik, J. (eds.) *Norsk matmakt i endring* (pp. 221–241). Bergen: Fagbokforlaget.

Hegnes, A. W. and Amilien, V. (2019) 'Geographical Indications – A Double-Edged Tool for Food Democracy: The Cases of the Norwegian Geographical Indication Evolution and the Protection of Stockfish from Lofoten as Cultural Adaptation Work', in Bonanno, A.,

Sekine, K. and Feuer H. N. (eds.) *Geographical Indication and Global Agri-Food: Development and Democratization* (pp. 100–117). New York: Routledge.

Muller, P., Böhm, M., Csillag, P., Donati, M., Drut, M., Ferrer-Pérez, H., Gauvrit, L., Gil, J.M., Hoang, V., Malak-Rawlikowska, A., Mattas, K., Napasin-tuwong, O., Nguyen, A., Papadopoulos, I., Ristic, B., Stojanovic, Z., Török, Á., Tsakiridou, E., Veneziani, M. and Bellassen, V. (2021) 'Are Certified Supply Chains More Socially Sustainable? A Bargaining Power Analysis', *Journal of Agricultural & Food Industrial Organization*, 19: 177–192.

Owen L., Udall D., Franklin, A. and Kneafsey, M. (2020) 'Place-Based Pathways to Sustainability: Exploring Alignment between Geographical Indications and the Concept of Agroecology Territories in Wales', *Sustainability* 12:1–25.

Richards, C., Bjørkhaug, H., Lawrence, G. and Hickman, E. (2013) 'Retailer-driven Agricultural Restructuring – Australia, the UK and Norway in Comparison', *Agriculture and Human Values* 30: 235–245.

Storstad, O. and Bjørkhaug, H. (2003) 'Foundations of Production and Consumption of Organic Food in Norway: Common Attitudes among Farmers and Consumers?', *Agriculture and Human Values,* 20: 151–163.

Vandecandelaere, E., Teyssier, C., Barjolle, D., Fournier, S., Beucherie, O and Jeanneaux P. (2020) 'Strengthening Sustainable Food Systems through Geographical Indications: Evidence from 9 Worldwide Case Studies', *Journal of Sustainability Research* 2(4): e200031.

Vittersø, G. and Tangeland, T. (2015) 'The Role of Consumers in Transitions Towards Sustainable Food Consumption. The Case of Organic Food in Norway', *Journal of Cleaner Production,* 92: 91–99.

Official Speeches

Sponheim, L. (2005) Trends and Development of Food from a Political Perspective. Presentation at the Brimi conference. Lom, September 21, 2005. (Trender and utvikling av mat sett fra et politisk miljø. Innlegg på Brimi-konferansen. Lom, 21. September 2005).

Øyangen, G. (1991) Strategies for Pure Food. Opening Speech at a Meeting with Organizations, Institutions, Companies, etc. Oslo, July 1st. (Strategier for rein mat. Innledningsforedrag på møte med organisasjoner, institusjoner, bedrifter mv. Oslo 1. juli).

Index

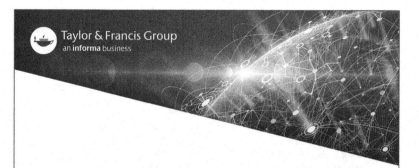

Printed in the United States
by Baker & Taylor Publisher Services